The PUPPY TRAINING

HANDBOOK

How to Raise The Dog of
Your Dreams

KAELIN MUNKELWITZ

ALL THINGS PUPS

PUBLISHING

. . . .

ALL THINGS PUPS PUBLICATIONS

WWW.ALLTHINGSPUPS.COM

First All Things Pups international mass market paperback edition, June 2017. The All Things Pups name and logo are trademarks of All Things Pups LLC. The publisher is not responsible for websites (or their content) that are not owned by the publisher.

LIBRARY OF CONGRESS CATALOGING-IN-PUBLICATION DATA

Munkelwitz, Kaelin
The Puppy Training Handbook / All Things Pups.
ISBN: 978-1544787633

Meet My Pups

JUNEAU & GRIZZLY

I will be constantly referring to my dogs throughout this book so I thought it best for you to meet them!

Meet Juneau!

Juneau is a three-year old Husky/German Shepherd mix. I adopted her from a rescue in Minnesota when she was eight weeks old. Juneau is my very bright, energetic, confident, and sassy girl. She is loyal to her people and LOVES being the center of attention. Juneau is OBSESSED with playing fetch. Luckily, Juneau's German Shepherd traits overrule the Husky traits when it comes to training, so she catches on right away and is very obedient.

Meet Grizzly!

Grizzly is one-year old and is the newest addition to the family! Grizzly was listed as a Lab mix when we adopted him, but we think he is a Newfoundland/Australian Shepherd mix. Grizzly was EXTREMELY shy and reserved when we first brought him home. He loved being around other dogs right from the start but didn't like humans. It has been so amazing to see him go from being so timid to watching him develop into a playful, obedient, and sweet pup who loves people! Grizzly is really mellow, hence why he's such a great temperament dog. He LOVES playing with his big sister, other dogs, and his toys.

TABLE OF CONTENTS

INTRODUCTION: TO A BETTER LIFE WITH YOUR PUP

⟩ SECTION 1 ⎸ THE PUPPY PREPARATION GAME-PLAN

> SECTION 2 | BRINGING YOUR PUPPY HOME —
> CREATING COMFORT

> SECTION 3 | HOW TO TRAIN YOUR DOG — TEACHING YOUR
> PUPPY TO LISTEN TO AND RESPECT YOUR COMMANDS

> SECTION 4 | SOLVING THE 20 TOUGHEST DOG
> BEHAVIORAL PROBLEMS

SECTION 5 | NECESSARY KNOWLEDGE FOR THE MOST DEDICATED DOG OWNERS

Introduction:
To a Better Life With
Your Pup

Welcome To a Better Life With Your Pup

Congratulations! You have just made the best decision you ever could make for your puppy: investing and engaging in the process of training him the right way. By the right way, I mean implementing the methods of training and care that are best for your individual pup. I am delighted to assist you on this exciting journey of developing a lifelong relationship with your dog through the content in this book.

Despite common claims of other training programs, there are no secrets to quickly or effectively train your dog. Rather, like a person, every dog has a different personality and genetic makeup based on breed that can create varying behaviors. I'm sick and tired of seeing generalized training books offering a one-size-fits-all approach— **Every dog is a unique soul who requires (and deserves!) special attention.** Therefore, I designed this extensive book to cater to the needs of individual puppy issues, while still providing an all-inclusive resource for dog owners of every age and experience level! **Whatever your needs are, I have them covered!**

Let's Start with a Little Soul Searching

The fact alone that you're reading this book proves to me that you care about your dog more than the large majority of dog owners out there.

The time you're spending reading these words, the excitement you possess to get started on the training process ahead, and the passion you have for your dog and giving them the best possible life, these are all things that make me so excited to help you raise and train the dog of your dreams!

But first, let's establish a sense of direction for you as you begin this journey. While the willingness to put in the time and work with passion is absolutely crucial to your success, what's just as important is your **intent and purpose.**

I can give you the best training methods, techniques, and tutorials in the world, but all of that means nothing if you aren't first asking yourself the tough questions that will give you a sense of purpose to strive for the results and the peace of mind that you want to achieve by training your dog.

🐾 WHAT DO YOU WANT?

Here is a question I ask <u>every</u> client of mine. Most dog owners lack a concrete answer, so I like to offer a few suggestions:

- Do you want a better-trained dog?
- Do you want a better relationship with your pup?
- Do you want to get rid of behavioral problems that are threatening the safety of others?
- Do you want to impress everyone with how well-behaved your dog is?
- Do you want to teach your pup cool tricks?
- Do you want to become a dog trainer?
- Do you just want to get better with dogs in general?

🐾 WHAT DO YOU *REALLY* WANT FOR YOUR DOG?

On hearing these suggestions, most dog owners still only muster "Yeah," or give a response that lacks conviction. They haven't decided what they want yet.

They're getting ready to embark upon a journey that will require them to work hard, swallow their pride, and take challenging steps to venture into a new passion, but they still haven't figured out why they're going to put in all that work!

That's why I ask my clients these pointed questions, and why I'm now asking YOU. I don't want you to get halfway through this book and say, "This sounds too hard. It's not worth all of the sacrifices." Instead, I want you to know what you want TODAY. Your goals will change as you learn more about your puppy, about canine behaviors, and how dogs' minds work, but you should always have an idea of what your objectives are. They will keep you focused when things get tough (such as if your puppy isn't being trained as quickly as you'd like), and keep you from getting too excited when you experience a small victory.

🐾 How *BAD* DO YOU WANT IT?

One of the greatest tragedies I see is how many dog owners give up too early, or never try at all. In fact, for many people, raising a puppy can be one of the hardest things they will ever learn. It WILL be an arduous journey; it WILL be emotionally draining; there most likely WILL be sleepless nights, and it WILL push you past your comfort zone to the cusp of your patience capacity. Why? Because you'll be challenging not just one aspect of yourself, but your true self, down to the core of your being. Training your dog is going to require:

🐾 PATIENCE: You'll be challenging your patience when things don't go as you planned — that little voice in the back of your head that's telling you, "Why is my puppy taking so long to learn this crap? I want a dog that actually listens to me."

🐾 FAITH: You'll be challenging your faith when you get frustrated – that little voice that keeps asking, "How long is this going to take? Will my puppy ever learn? Should I just give up?"

🐾 HABITS: You'll be challenging your current and past habits — whether those are going to the bars every weekend or leaving your residence for several hours or days at a time, you will have to make sacrifices in the early weeks and months of your dog's life so that he can properly develop and become comfortable under your care.

How To Successfully Use This Book

To make this learning process as clear as possible, I have designed this guide to include symbols that keep you aware of critical points. Keep an eye out for these important points throughout this book:

KEYS TO SUCCESS

The key symbol means that I want to reiterate important points that will set you up for success. These are strategies that I believe will help you become the best puppy parent you can be.

BRIGHT IDEAS

The light bulb symbol indicates a tip that will improve your approach to raising and training your pup.

Look at the resources in this book as pieces of a puzzle, with the finished picture being your well-trained and happy pup. Every dog owner has a different picture of what they want for their pup, so I can't define this for you. However, what I *can* do is provide you with the expert knowledge, tools, and strategies you need to fulfill your puppy dreams in whatever area of puppy parenthood you need help. To do so, here are two ways you can fill in your puppy's puzzle:

1

Fill in the pieces you need most using specific sections in this Handbook (Advanced dog owners ONLY)

Some dog owners I come across have simple goals for raising their puppy. For instance, if you DREAM of having a dog that will simply come when he is called and sit when he is commanded to, then use these pieces of the puzzle to train your dog to do just those things. Or, if you are an advanced dog owner, and your pup already has a training foundation imprinted into his behaviors, then pick and choose the sections in this handbook you feel would complete the puzzle of your ideal dog.

> While this strategy gives you more freedom, I suggest adhering to this book's full method, which ensures that you're raising your pup into a happy, healthy and well-trained dog. Years of experience in the dog-training field have taught me that it is *better to follow a proven strategy completely than to pick individual pieces on your own.*

2

Implement the teachings in this book step-by-step to mold your puppy into a well-trained member of your family (Strongly Recommended).

While the first method may fit your needs if you are an advanced owner, following this book's strategies in the order they're written will give you the best preparation to effectively and efficiently raise your puppy. Instead of trying to pick and choose which pieces you feel your dog needs most, rely on the expertise of my years of experience to guide you through puppy parenthood step-by-step as we fill in the puzzle of your puppy's foundation TOGETHER! Don't worry about missing a thing, as I will guide you through every important checkpoint of properly raising a happy and healthy dog.

As you embark on the puppy parenthood journey, feel free to refer to earlier points in the book to refresh your memory on certain points. This handbook is meant to be a guide that you return to often! Don't treat it as another book that you read through once and then cast it to the depths of your library, never to be read again.

Again, **in order to get the most out of this book, I strongly encourage you to refer back to it often.** If you don't do this, you are selling yourself short and truly limiting how much you and your pup can grow together.

The Hard Truth About Raising a Pup: What You NEED To Know

When it comes to raising a pup, many first-time dog owners vastly underestimate the commitment they will have to give to raise and train their pup successfully.

Q *Why?*

Well, the sad reality is that many dog trainers will mislead you to believe that training your pup will be easy just to get you to buy their product.

The truth is that while the process of training a dog is indeed simple once learned, it is by no means easy.

As the saying goes, nothing worth having in life comes easy, and unfortunately, this applies to raising your dog as well. However, many dog owners, misled by the hegemonic dogma of money-hungry dog trainers, will embody the mindset that raising and training their puppy will be "easy." They'll try it out for a little while, only to get discouraged by initial failure and decide, "Oh, this isn't for me," or, "This might work for other people, but it won't work for me because..." They throw in the towel days or weeks later due to a myriad of excuses such as:

"It's too hard to train a puppy," or
"I don't have enough time," or,
"It's too much work to take care of him."

As an avid rescue supporter, I'm a huge advocate of educating people who think like this before they get to this point of surrender and quit on their dog.

This is, unfortunately, a common outcome for people who have a distorted vision of what dog ownership looks like, people who made a decision without being prepared for the consequences.

But there's no need to worry, that's not going to happen to you!

I'm going to prepare you for every hurdle or speed bump you may encounter as a new puppy owner. Before I show you what to do, there is an important ideological foundation to describe to you that lies underneath the principles of this book. This next section sets the ideological basis of this book, as it describes the process of achieving successful puppy parenthood.

As with all things in life, when it all comes down to it, there are two paths to success:

- 🐕 Work Hard
- 🐕 Work Smart

Most people do neither, and have no success. Some people take one of those paths, and have some success. A few people — a very small minority — do both, and have CRAZY success.

In this book, I'm going to ask you to do both.

★ THE WORK SMART part of the formula is this book — your guide for the road ahead to effectively raise your puppy into a happy member of your family. Refer to it often, do the things it tells you to do, and make sure you're implementing everything it states. Each piece of information I'm providing is a key piece in the puzzle; miss or skip a few, and you still might be able to make out the picture, but it will not be the one you envisioned.

Start at the beginning and work your way through in order. I start with the basics and build into more advanced information. And when you find you're hitting a stumbling block — that there's some obstacle in your way that's making it difficult to advance — stop, go through this book again, and pinpoint what you're missing, or what you could be doing better.

★ THE WORK HARD part of the formula is you getting out there and doing it. If you want to learn how to train and raise your dog the right way, you HAVE to deliberately and continuously practice the principles delivered in this book. No dog owner has or will ever become good with dogs by just reading a book, trying to teach their pup a few tricks and then giving up. Teaching your new puppy positive behaviors needs to become a consistent habit. Just as you should go to the gym four to five days a week if you want to get in shape, or, if you want to be a good writer, you have to write a minimum of a few thousand words a day, the same principle of consistent work ethic applies to training your dog.

★ YOU MUST WORK TO GET THE RESULTS THAT YOU WANT.

No one can do it for you! What kind of results can you get? It depends on you: how driven you are, how committed you are to your goals, and how willing you are to change. I've seen puppy owners who were passionate about dogs and just needed to advance their strategies, and I've seen owners who struggled for longer, with limited success here and there, before finally breaking through and developing the relationship they always dreamed of having with their dog.

Which leads me to one more important principle: **Just as in life, often the dog owners who find real success are the ones who reach the point of giving up and forge on ahead anyway.** The winners say, "Screw it," and keep swinging until they hit something, no matter how many misses they already have. The winners are the ones who push past all the obstacles on the road to success. They don't care how long the road may be; they are on a mission and won't let anything stop them from achieving the proverbial mountaintop.

🐾 TO GET TO THE PUNCH LINE, THERE ARE REALLY ONLY TWO FACTORS THAT WILL DETERMINE THE SUCCESS OR FAILURE OF THE TRAINING YOU LEARN IN THIS BOOK:

1

The Amount Of Reinforcement And Work You Actually Put Into The Training.

A huge tenant of my training philosophy that I stress to every dog owner is that one session with me won't magically turn your dog into a well-behaved dog.

> *You are going to have to put in the work to reinforce the tools and techniques that I give you.*

There is no magic pill to train your dog; there are no 'secrets' or gimmicks that will help you accomplish it quicker and easier than everybody else. There are no shortcuts. There are no hacks. Raising a dog well is a learning process, one that anyone can succeed at if they work smart AND hard. Your success is only limited by how willing you are to do the work.

If you only reinforce the methods I give you half of the time, you should only expect to see half of the potential results.

Q *Isn't this something that applies to every area of life?*

If you only put 50% into your workouts at the gym, you shouldn't expect to be in the very best shape possible for you to be.

If you only study for half of the subjects on your test, you can't expect to receive 100% on every subject.

We all know this life lesson and it is no different when applying it to training your dog.

2

Patience When Working Through The Dog's Individual Learning Threshold.

Dogs do indeed have different intelligence levels and some catch on to different training concepts faster than others. When you combine this reality with impatient owners in today's society, a lot of people end up quitting on their dogs!

However, if you are consistent in reinforcing the training, your dog (no matter what his intelligence level may be) WILL catch on.

Ultimately, my clients who put in 100% effort and consistency, see 100% improvement and results with their dogs.

I can give you the best tools in the world, but it won't matter if you aren't willing to put in the consistent work over the long-term.

Another thing people always ask me is:

"Has there ever been a dog you weren't able to train?"

I love answering this question!

The 100% truth is I have never worked with a dog who has not responded nor improved after being exposed to my positive reinforcement training methods. There are, however, people who don't see the results they want because of one of two reasons:

A. They don't reinforce and build upon the foundation we set in our training sessions.

B. They aren't patient enough to work with their dog's individual ability to learn and develop new behavior based on their unique genetics and environment.

That, my friends, is the **only** difference between my clients who succeed in raising a well-behaved and trained dog, and those who fall short.

Training a well-behaved and well-trained dog takes PATIENCE.

Patience will be your number one tool to fall back on when training your dog; it may also be the most challenging part of training.

This is where most people stumble, and where you, as the owner, have to work on. Our society has taught us the false pretense that there is such thing as an "overnight success"; that you can become successful at something without working hard.

I think this is one of the main reasons why it's so hard for most people to work through behavioral issues with their dogs... Because 90% of us are impatient as hell and want an obedient dog without putting in the work that it requires!

So, my friends, please keep the universal key of patience at the forefront of your mind throughout this journey that you're about to embark on, as it may play a very important role in the ultimate success or failure of your training goals. The choice is yours!

Where To Start?

SIT DOWN AND BEGIN WRITING OUT YOUR GOALS FOR
YOUR PUPPY'S TRAINING.

- Do you want your puppy to immediately come when he is called?
- Do you want to be able to bring your dog out in public without worrying about him misbehaving?
- Do you want your dog to be able to do tricks like "shake" and "touch" on command?
- Do you want your puppy to become your best friend, emotional rock, and an important member of your family for years to come?

Write down everything that you want, no matter how big or small the goal.

Put your list somewhere you will see it regularly (such as your bathroom mirror). Look at it at least twice a day — once in the morning when you wake up, and once at night before you go to bed. And every time you do, ask yourself, "Will today (or did today, if it's in the PM) get me closer to meeting my goals?" At the end of the day, if you didn't do what you set out to do, ask yourself, "What can I do better next time to ensure that I'm staying on track?"

Keys to Success

Write down your puppy parenthood goals, post them in a place you'll see them often (such as your bathroom mirror), and look at them at least twice a day to make sure you're on track.

How To Raise The Dog
Of Your Dreams

❯ SECTION 1 | THE PUPPY PREPARATION GAME PLAN

The first section in this book outlines general preparation guidelines that apply to almost every puppy and dog owner, laying out a practical process to help you effectively prepare for your new pup. This section includes expert knowledge on the following: how to prepare for your puppy, budgeting for your pup, and outlining the materials and products mandatory to ensure success in the training process.

❯ SECTION 2 | BRINGING YOUR PUPPY HOME — CREATING COMFORT

Next I'll walk you through arguably the most exciting yet also the most stressful part of getting a new pup: bringing your puppy home. Feel more at ease with this uncertain transition by learning about the protocol for bringing your puppy home, what to expect during the first

72 hours, and immediately getting your pup acclimated to a feeding schedule.

› SECTION 3 | HOW TO TRAIN YOUR DOG — TEACHING YOUR PUPPY TO HEAR, RESPOND AND LISTEN TO YOUR COMMANDS

This section illustrates one of the most important areas of dog parenting that usually presents the largest obstacles for new dog owners: teaching your dog to listen to you and respond to your commands. This step-by-step section clears up common training misconceptions and provides you with a simple training progression that will help you masterfully gain higher levels of respect and obedience from your pup.

› SECTION 4 | SOLVING THE 20 TOUGHEST DOG BEHAVIORAL PROBLEMS

This hands-on section provides detailed training corrections of the most common behavioral problems dog owners may encounter. From simple solutions such as pulling on the leash to urgent issues such as aggression, this portion of the book will cover just about every behavioral problem possible and provides step-by-step details on how to manage these specific issues that you may encounter as a dog owner.

› SECTION 5 | NECESSARY KNOWLEDGE FOR THE MOST DEDICATED DOG OWNERS

In this last section, I'm going to give you basic and advanced dog knowledge that will put you ahead of the game not only for raising a happy puppy, but a happy, adult dog — while saving you headaches and dollars in the process! Whether you're still preparing yourself for puppy parenthood or you've successfully implemented the earlier sections of this book, the information in the last section gives you invaluable knowledge that will complete your puppy's "puzzle." Get ready to learn about socializing your puppy, grooming needs, and basic veterinary knowledge to wrap up this comprehensive puppy parenthood guide. What are you waiting for? Go ahead and dive in!

THE PUPPY PREPARATION GAME PLAN

PREPARING FOR YOUR PUP

About to adopt or purchase a new pup?

I hope you are deciding to adopt! :)

Sit down and get ready to take some notes; this section is vital if you wish to successfully raise a dog. Whether you have yet to pick out your newest family member or you're counting down the days until it's time to bring your dog home, preparing for your dog BEFORE the dog arrives is one of the most important things you can do as a new dog owner. Following these guidelines for preparation will make your life tremendously easier once your dog arrives.

❧ RESEARCH YOUR PUPPY'S BREED

Before bringing your puppy home, you should definitely do a lot of research on your pup's breed(s). Every breed is SO different and comes with its own set of needs. From grooming to energy level capacities to behavioral traits and more, you should have a basic understanding of what to expect for your dog. What you learn may impact your purchasing decisions, how you prepare your home for your puppy's arrival, and how you approach its training.

Behaviors vary an incredible amount between breeds, and you may need to use different training tactics depending on your puppy's behavior and personality. After researching your dog's breed in detail (or, if you haven't chosen your puppy yet, research the breed of your choice and see if the dog's needs fit your personality and lifestyle), continue to the budgeting section.

🐾 Budgeting For Your Pup

Are you truly prepared to raise a puppy? DO NOT overlook the financials.

One of the biggest mistakes new dog owners make is adopting a new dog WITHOUT properly budgeting for the multitude of recurring costs that adding a pet to the family will generate. If this is you, then don't worry! Starting a budget late is better than never budgeting at all, so take action NOW since preparing financially for your pup is crucial to your long term success or failure as a puppy parent.

> ### KEYS TO SUCCESS
>
> Preparing for the financial commitment that your pup requires is CRUCIAL to your long term success as a puppy parent.

🐾 How much should I expect to spend
IN THE FIRST YEAR?

I get this question a lot from serious dog owners, and the honest answer is that only YOU can answer that for yourself. Every prospective puppy parent enters this situation with different personal goals and infinite possibilities that could occur in their first year of raising a puppy. Therefore, instead of trying to come up with a broad answer to this important question — as taking into account each person's and pup's individual situations would be nearly impossible — I have developed **The Puppy Financial Planner** so that you can see for yourself. Read through the rest of this section about The Puppy Preparation Checklist, then create a mock budget for yourself (plugging in the adoption/purchase fee, food, treats, crate, etc.) to see how much the first year of puppy parenthood will cost for you!

Now, these estimates are assuming that your dog is healthy and does not need additional medical services. If they do encounter any health-related issues, you can plan for that by putting a higher value in the Veternarian Visits section of The Puppy Financial Planner.

On that note, it is very wise to look into obtaining pet insurance or have money tucked away specifically for a pet emergency. Veterinary bills are NOT cheap. Trust me, something can happen when you least expect it; and just like in your personal life, you want to be financially prepared for the unexpected.

THE PUPPY FINANCIAL PLANNER

Plan how much the first year of puppy parenthood will cost:

Product/Item	Cost	x	# of Purchases/ Year	=	Cost/ Year
Adoption/Purchase Fee					
Kennel/Crate					
Dog Bed					
Food					
Toys					
Treats					

Medications (Flea & Tick, Heartworm, etc.)					
Veterinarian Visits					
Misc. Costs					
ESTIMATED TOTAL COST OF FIRST YEAR					

The Puppy Preparation Checklist

.... 🐾 ....

The next step in preparation is to purchase the items you will need for your puppy right away. **Refer to the checklist below for the items you should purchase BEFORE bringing your puppy home:**

PUPPY PREPARATION CHECKLIST	
Crate	☐
Dog Food	☐
Food and Water bowls	☐
Training Treats	☐
Toys	☐
Chewing Items	☐

Collar, Harness, and Leash	☐
Baby Gates (Optional)	☐
Brush	☐
Dog Toothbrush/Toothpaste	☐
Ear Cleaning Solution	☐
Dog Shampoo	☐
Dog Nail Clippers	☐
Poop Bags	☐
Treat Pouch/Carrier	☐
First Aid Supplies	☐
Heartworm/Flea/Tick Preventative	☐

BRIGHT IDEAS

Use this checklist in concert with "The Puppy Financial Planner" and the descriptions below to help you estimate how much the first year of puppy parenthood will cost you.

❧ CRATE:

I can't stress enough the importance of a puppy having his own crate. It's at the top of this list for the following reasons:

1. **Dogs are den animals and need a space of their own to feel safe and secure.** It is essential for their well-being that every dog has his own little safe place where he can relax.

2. **It is great for your pup's mind and all-around behavior.** Puppies are distracted very easily, and your house is full of a million distracting things that will pull your pup's attention this way and that. When puppies are roaming around freely in a distracting environment, their minds are constantly racing: "What can I chew on next? What can I get into next?" The crate is the one area that you can limit any distractions and allow your pup's curious mind to take a break.

3. **It is crucial for the dog to have a crate in order to be properly house trained.** Your puppy's crate will be the one place where you can be assured that he will not have an accident (as long as the crate isn't too large and you do not leave him inside for longer than he can physically hold it). Dogs instinctively will not go to the bathroom where they sleep or where they deem their "den area" to be.

When choosing the right crate, keep in mind that the size of the dog's crate is extremely important! A crate that is too small is a problem for the obvious reason that the dog will be uncomfortable. No one would want to be squished inside of a room that they could barely lie down in.

However, it is also a very common mistake for dog owners to use a crate that is too large for their puppy. When the puppy has too much room in his crate, he no longer thinks of the entire crate as a den. If the puppy has room to walk around in the crate, the puppy will think of one area of the crate as his den, and the other will be used as a zone to go potty in. **Yes, that's right, if a dog has a crate that is too large, he or she will go to the bathroom inside of it.** However, when a crate is just the right size, a dog will not want to make his or her safe place dirty and will not want to go to the bathroom inside of the crate.

4. **It is a crucial training tool for self-control and boundary training.**

   As you'll read later in this book, the crate can also be used as a "control area" to train desirable behaviors and work through severe behavioral issues such as separation anxiety.

Q WHAT KIND OF CRATE SHOULD I PURCHASE?

There are two main options for crates: wire or plastic. Although there are advantages and disadvantages to both types, **I suggest a wire crate** for a number of reasons. For one thing, wire crates will offer a divider feature that allows you to start small when your puppy comes home and adjust the size of the space as he grows. That way you can use the same crate for the dog's entire life.

With plastic crates, you will have to purchase new ones as the dog outgrows his space. For those on a strict budget, this makes the decision to invest in a quality wire crate a better long-term investment.

> Obviously, some puppies can be larger than other full grown dogs depending on the breed, so make sure to figure out what size crate will fit your puppy when he is fully grown (based on his breed(s).

Wire crates are a lot easier to maneuver, too, because they collapse and fold, whereas plastic crates do not. Wire crates have a removable tray at the bottom, so they are very easy to clean. And, in my experience, I think that most dogs are happier being in a wire crate because they can see outside of it a lot better than when they are in a plastic crate.

Really, the only advantage of a plastic crate is that they are designed to be able to transport your pet – something you are not able to do with a wire crate, which is not airline-approved.

Having said all of that, the choice is still yours to make. I have used both wire and plastic crates, and they have both been effective tools to train and provide a dog with a safe place of his own. Choose whichever crate best fits your personal needs.

❧ Dog Food:

I'd like to pre-empt this section by noting that I'm not a pet nutrition-ist and don't have a background in this field. With that being said, I have a ton of experience in the dog industry and LOTS of smart friends in the pet nutrition field who have educated me consider-ably about the ins and outs of dog nutrition, to the point where I feel confident providing you with ideas and opinions derived from my own experience successfully helping others raise happy and healthy dogs.

The first principle to understand regarding nutrition is just how crucial it is for a puppy's development that he eats food that will give him a complete and balanced diet! Not only will it impact your pup's energy and happiness, but it's also imperative in helping him live a long and healthy life. One has to be very cautious as there is a lot of harmful food being sold that is causing irreparable harm, which is why I BEG you to educate yourself about what you're really feeding your dog before feeding him something that will hurt him over the long term.

It's crazy to me how similar the parallels are between dog nutrition and dog training; just as a lack of education and misinformation has led many dog owners to go down the wrong path when training their dog, the same goes for those same owners when they go to the store to feed their pup.

🐾 WHAT KIND OF FOOD SHOULD I BE FEEDING MY DOG?

The two main options I recommend are raw feeding and high quality, grain-free kibble.

·············· *Raw Feeding* ··············

When you think of the healthiest type of food for humans, what first comes to mind? Food that is all-natural and not processed, right?

Well, the same goes for dogs. A raw, all-natural, non-processed, and carnivorous diet is the healthiest option to feed your dog.

Dogs are carnivores that possess the digestive system, stomach acid, and the bacteria killing means to eat raw meat and raw bones, which offer higher vital nutrient and mineral content than cooked meat, and a long list of other health benefits that go on and on.

Since the ingredients in a raw diet are never cooked or altered from their natural state, it is easier for a dog's digestive system to assimilate and utilize all of the nutrients in the food that are vital to their health.

If you have the time and the financial means to feed your dog raw food, then I highly recommend this option. To figure out what kind of a raw diet is best for your dog, I suggest talking with a pet nutritionist at your local holistic pet store.

High Quality & Grain-Free Kibble

With dry kibble, there are hundreds of options to choose from. To make the selection process easier on you, I recommend considering these points to ensure that your pup is getting the best nutrition possible:

- Higher quality dry kibble is definitely worth the cost compared to cheaper dry kibble. If you really dig into the science behind cheap kibble, you will never want to feed it to your dogs ever again. If you're looking for more information on this, I recommend watching the documentary "Pet Fooled", which exposes the pet food industry's inner workings and corruption.

  - High-quality dry kibble ensures that the dog is obtaining a complete and balanced nutrition and that he will live a longer, healthier life.

- Stay away from colored kibble, which is clear evidence of food coloring that is harmful for your dog.

- Make sure you know each ingredient in the food that you'll be feeding your dog.

- Stick to a grain-free diet.

  - I have found that grain-free food is easiest on dog's stomachs and that dogs really do not need grain in their diet.

  - Grain is the most common allergen in dog foods.

Before I had Juneau on a grain-free diet, she was constantly itching herself. I tried a variety of different things to help her itching, and ultimately it was switching her to a grain-free food that resolved the issue.

- Only shop at local holistic pet stores for your dog's food and treats.

- I've found that these smaller Mom and Pop stores have a different sense of purpose that focuses more on the individual dog and providing the best nutrition based on your dog's needs.

🐾 Some dogs are very sensitive to dog food and may need to be on a hypoallergenic diet.

- Finding out if a type of food is right for your dog is basically just trial and error, and a dog's stool is the best indicator.

- Changing dog foods is hard on a dog's stomach, so it is best to stick to one kind.

  ★ If you do have to switch up the dog's food, I recommend mixing the new food with the old food for a couple of days before switching to the new food completely.

🐾 Through my experience I have found the following four brands to be my favorites:

- **NutriSource** (A really good, high-quality brand for people with multiple dogs or anyone who is on a budget but still wants their dog to have excellent nutrition.)

- **Stella & Chewy's** (A bit more expensive but very nutrient dense and rich in crucial vitamins.)

- **PureVita** (Engineered specially for dogs with allergies and sensitivities.)

- **Open Farm** (definitely on the more expensive end but they grow and raise all of their own ingredients.)

When you are bringing your new pup home, make sure to find out what kind of dog food the puppy has been eating and see if you can take some of that food with you when you pick him up. That way, for the first couple days you can mix the old food with your puppy's new food to make it an easier transition on the puppy's stomach.

❧ Food and Water Bowls:

When it comes to food and water bowls, **I recommend any kind except for those made out of plastic.** Why? I can almost guarantee that your puppy will chew the plastic bowls. You will end up with destroyed bowls and possibly a puppy who has swallowed plastic pieces. Not good on both ends!

❧ Training Treats:

You are going to need A LOT of training treats. I recommend soft treats, instead of hard, that you can break into tiny pieces. Sojo's 100% raw freeze-dried, are my favorite training treats. They come in multiple delicious flavors, dogs LOVE them, and you can feel confident about their nutrition since they are ONE high quality ingredient!

The NutriSource grain-free soft treats are also great. They come in a variety of flavors, are easy to break into smaller pieces, and most importantly — are made from a trustworthy brand that cares about your pet's nutrition.

❧ TOYS:

You will need a lot of dog toys, of course! When it comes to toys, just be sure that the toys you buy for your puppy are specifically for dogs. Manufacturers of dog toys know that these toys will be in dogs' mouths and use appropriate materials to make them. Stuffed animals meant for children, for example, may be stuffed with a different filling that has chemicals that could be harmful to dogs. Manufacturers of children's toys do not presume that their products will be ripped apart and chewed on; dog toy makers treat it as a given. More often than not, children's stuffed animals are safe for dogs, but just play it safe and buy toys that are specifically designed for dogs.

The most important thing about dog toys is that **your pup should ALWAYS be monitored when playing with a toy.** Dogs, especially puppies, have a tendency to chew and destroy toys (or anything they can get their mouths on!) Puppies like to rip toys apart, which can lead to them trying to eat the small bits that result. Many dog toys also consist of items that are not meant to be swallowed such as fabric, stuffing, squeakers, rope, or plastic. I have seen far too many pups have to undergo a foreign body removal surgery from eating large of pieces of destroyed toys. For this reason, when your puppy is playing with a toy, you need to be monitoring him the entire time. And the same goes for in the crate, never leave a puppy alone with a toy in there! If you do want to leave an item in there to keep him entertained when alone, refer to the following section.

❧ CHEWING ITEMS:

The chewing items that I recommend below are safe to leave alone with your puppy in his kennel. Giving your puppy chewing items in his kennel can also significantly help with the crate training process.

Q *What types of chewing items are beneficial for my puppy?*

There are a lot of different types of acceptable chewing objects for puppies. **Chewing objects are essential for puppies, as dogs actually have a need for chewing, just as they have for eating and exercising.** Also, chewing objects benefit the health of your dog's teeth and gums and can provide him with healthy minerals. Chewing objects are also essential tools for training as they can be used for directing your pup to appropriate items to chew on, and will keep him from chewing on inappropriate things such as the furniture.

Here are the chewing objects that I recommend:

Antlers

Antlers are hands down the most amazing chewing object for dogs. They are full of vitamins and minerals, they are natural, and they last FOREVER. ('Forever' in dog language means a few months.)

Q *Why are they so great?*

For one, **they are much safer than any other chewing item because they are a lot less likely to break off into pieces or splinter.** Also, antlers will keep your pup busy for a long time, while providing him with health benefits. Antlers are a little bit more pricey, but I promise you they are worth it.

Bully Sticks

Bully sticks are another great choice. They don't last nearly as long as antlers but last quite a bit longer than other chewing treats. Dogs absolutely love them. They will only last a day or two but will keep your puppy busy for a little while. They are natural and also full of vitamins and minerals for your pup. I recommend purchasing the odorless bully sticks, as they can get pretty smelly!

Himalayan Dog Chews

Himalayan dog chews are a healthy chewing object made primarily from Yak's milk. (It sounds funny, I know.) Himalayan chews keep a dog entertained for quite some time and fulfill his need to chew. They last longer than a bully stick, but not as long as an antler.

Q *What about bones?*

All chewing objects have pros and cons, so I advise you to watch your puppy carefully when he is chewing on any object. While I recommend purchasing bones for your puppy, **you must be very careful with what kind of bones you choose.** Bones can be very beneficial for your pup, but they can also be detrimental, even deadly.

Q *What types of bones do you recommend?*

I only recommend bones that are:

- **Organic**
- **Made in the United States**
- **Raw**

I am strict about organic bones because you need to know that the products you are giving your puppy are all natural. Foreign bones and other items can be deadly to your dog if he consumes something that is toxic or artificially created. That's why I also recommend you only buy American-made. Other countries don't have nearly as strict regulations as the U.S. when making dog and other animal products.

Toxic chemicals have consistently been found on chewing objects for dogs made outside of the United States.

> **Q** *What kinds of bones are harmful to my pup?*

- **Cooked Bones**

DO NOT EVER GIVE YOUR PUPPY COOKED BONES!
Cooked bones can splinter very easily, which can cause an irreparable amount of internal damage. The splintered bones can get lodged in your puppy's esophagus or severely injure the stomach. A puppy who has splintered bones in his body will most likely need surgery to remove them. Not fun!

- **Rawhide Bones**

Rawhide bones are the most common type of bone that you will find at any large pet store. However, I strongly recommend against ever purchasing this kind of bone.

> **Q** *Well, why are they so widely sold? And why shouldn't I use them?*

Rawhide is so commonly purchased by naive dog owners for two reasons:

1. **It is cheap.**
2. **People don't know any better.**

What a vast majority of puppy and dog owners DON'T know is it's very easy for a puppy to bite off a large piece of rawhide and swallow it whole. This is dangerous because **rawhide isn't digestible for a puppy and can cause gastrointestinal problems or blockage**, which means surgery for your pup and a ridiculously high vet bill coming your way. Still, want to buy rawhide? I didn't think so.

BRIGHT IDEAS

Refrain from giving your puppy cooked and rawhide bones when purchasing chewing items. Instead, stick with organic bones, bully sticks and antlers.

🐾 COLLAR, HARNESS, AND LEASH:

As for collars, harnesses, and leashes, there are a variety of different types to choose from. **For puppies, starting off with a simple collar and leash is completely fine.** If your puppy is still very young, chances are he hasn't even been on a walk with a collar and leash yet, so the first step will be getting him comfortable with the feeling of a collar and walking on a leash. However, keep in mind that you're going to end up buying 2-4 collars over your dog's lifetime, depending on how fast your puppy grows.

Collar

Q *What type of collar should I purchase?*

There are a variety of collars you can buy, and different styles serve different purposes. However, out of the four options listed below, I recommend sticking with one of the first two.

🐕 Simple Collar

- The simple collar is the most common collar you will see on dogs. It's flat and connects with a clip or buckle.

- **I recommend starting with this collar for your puppy.**

  ★ If your pup has no issue walking on the leash and isn't pulling, you can continue to use the simple collar.

🐾 Martingale Collar

- **The Martingale Collar is hands-down my favorite training collar.**

- It was designed so that your pup isn't able to slip out of the collar.

  - ★ It gently tightens around the neck when your dog is pulling on the leash as well, which is a great added training bonus to encourage loose leash walking.

🐾 Choke Collar

- **I DO NOT recommend the choke collar.**

  - ★ It can be very harmful to a dog when used incorrectly, which in most cases it is.

  - ★ Most of the time people pull way too hard on this collar, which can injure your dog's neck.

  - ★ Dogs will respond better to a gentle tug on their collar rather than a choke. *Stay away from these.*

🐾 Prong Collar

- **I personally do not recommend prong collars.**

  - ★ I don't believe that pinching your dog is the right way to teach him how to walk on a leash.

- Prong collars are not always effective, and often the dog will associate the negative pinching feeling with other things around him, such as another dog or animal, which can escalate aggression.

- With the other options of collars and harnesses available, there is really no need for the prong collar.

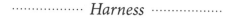

Harness

Dog owners often overlook harnesses. **However, harnesses can be one of the most amazing tools for teaching your pup to walk on a leash properly.** Despite my best efforts, Juneau was constantly pulling on the leash as a puppy and introducing her to a harness was the best choice I made.

Harnesses help immensely with pulling, taking all the unwanted pressure off of the pup's neck, and giving you more control of your dog's entire body. *They are amazing!*

Q *What type of harness should I purchase?*

There are two basic types of harnesses: ones that are chest-led and ones that clip on the dog's back.

🐕 Chest-led harnesses

- **Chest-led harnesses are the most effective type of harness.**

- These harnesses allow you to have directional control and make it very difficult for your pup to be able to pull you.

- How, you may ask? The leash is connected to a ring connected to a double-martingale on the chest, which deters the dog from pulling, and instead, guides your pup to back to you.

🐕 Back-clipping harnesses

- This type of harness is designed so that the leash attaches to a ring on top of the dog's back.

- **Back-clipping Harnesses can be a good tool, *depending on the dog.***

- The drawback of this type of harness is that it doesn't allow you to have complete directional control and will not be as effective in correcting a dog's pulling issues.

  - ★ While your pup will not be able to pull as much as with a collar, he certainly can pull more than he could with a chest-led harness.

- If your pup doesn't have a pulling issue and you are just simply looking to alleviate all of the pressure off his neck, this harness will work wonderfully.

·········· *Leash* ··········

There are two main types of leashes: standard and retractable. I recommend a standard leash for <u>all</u> puppy and dog owners.

Q *What are the differences between these types?*

STANDARD LEASHES:

🐕 Standard leashes are usually made out of nylon and sometimes leather.

🐕 They typically range from four to eight feet long and hook onto your pup's collar or harness.

Some guidelines for choosing the right standard leash:

🐕 **Choose a leash that is *no longer* than six feet long.**

- This gives your pup more than enough slack to walk properly on a leash but doesn't give him enough room to have freedom and roam around as he pleases. I prefer leashes that are only four feet long.

🐕 **Make sure that the handle is comfortable for you.**

- You are going to be holding this quite often, so you want to make sure it is not going to be painful for you to hold for extended periods of time.

  * Depending on the person, some materials or sizes of handles aren't comfortable on people's hands.

KEYS TO SUCCESS

If you're looking for a quick answer on collar, harness and leash options, my favorite combination of items for training puppies is the martingale collar, chest-led harness and standard leash.

RETRACTABLE LEASHES:

I *strongly* discourage dog owners from using retractable leashes.

🔑 Retractable leashes have large plastic handles that retract very long **nylon** cords.

🔑 These leashes aren't beneficial in training your dog and actually can be very harmful to you and your pup.

🔑 I can't even begin to tell you how many horror stories I've heard about people injuring themselves or their dogs when using this type of leash.

🔑 Unfortunately, many dog owners have not been educated about the dangers of using these leashes, and they are still popular today.

Reasons why I strongly discourage using a retractable leash:

🔑 **They don't train your dog how to properly walk on a leash.**

- Retractable leashes are confusing for dogs because the distance they are allowed to go is always changing. He will always test the leash to see how far he can go which will end up encouraging him to pull.

🐾 **They allow way too much freedom to roam.**

- Leash walking should train your pup to stay close to you.

🐾 **Retractable leashes can be dangerous for YOU.**

- Many people have received a rope burn or sliced hands from attempting to grab onto the leash.

- The thin nylon cord can slice into your skin, and it's extremely painful.

🐾 **Retractable leashes can be dangerous for YOUR PUP.**

- Your puppy can easily get tangled up in the cord.

- If he gets tangled up and then tries pull away, it will cause the rope to tighten even more, and it can lead to a serious accident.

- If the rope gets tangled around the dog's neck, *it can be fatal.*

For these reasons I suggest you stay FAR away from retractable leashes. Nothing good comes from them!

🐾 BABY GATES (OPTIONAL)

If there are certain areas of your house that you don't want your dog in, you may want to set up baby gates. Your pup will get into whatever he can, so be prepared to block off those areas of your home. It is a lot easier for a dog to understand that he isn't allowed somewhere if it is blocked off than to tell the puppy "no" and redirect him.

Using a crate is the most effective way to accomplish this; it creates a control or "den area" where your pup can calm his energy as well as learn boundaries and structure. For those of you who don't want to use a crate, baby gates can sometimes be used as a substitute for the dog's "den area". If your dog is having accidents in the house but you don't want to use a crate, you can create a control area using a baby gate to block off a small area of your home to establish boundaries. However, keep in mind that your dog still may have accidents if the control area is too large, which is another reason why I recommend using a crate in the first place.

🐾 BRUSH

Brushing your dog is very important, no matter the length of his coat. Yes, even dogs with extremely short hair— Boxers and Pitbulls, for example— need to be brushed. Refer to the "Brushing Fur" part of Section 5 for more information about why every dog needs to be brushed.

The type of brush used on your dog should be determined by the length and texture of your dog's coat. There are a variety of different types of brushes that are designed for specific types of fur.

🐾 Bristle Brush

- **Designed for short-haired dogs.**

- This brush has natural, closely packed bristles.

  ★ The bristles will help to pick up loose fur and stimulate the skin.

🐾 Slicker Brush

- **Designed for medium-to-long-haired or curly-haired dogs.**

- This brush consists of thin, wire pins on a flat surface.

★ The pins help to remove tangles and mats, while also picking up loose fur and stimulating the skin.

🐾 Pin Brush

- **Designed for long-haired dogs.**

- This brush looks similar to human brushes, usually oval with wire pins that are topped with small plastic rubber and are spread further apart than slicker brush pins.

- Used to detangle long hair and fluff an already well-brushed coat.

- This brush is also used to finish the grooming process and should be used along with a slicker brush.

🐾 Rake Brush

- **Designed for short, medium, and long-haired dogs.**

- This brush is made up of two rows of closely packed, thicker pins and resembles the look of a razor.

- Used to pick up loose fur, undercoat, rat out mats, and stimulate the skin.

- This kind of brush is very useful when a dog is shedding.

- Be extra sure to use the correct sized brush with this type— the pins should be about the same length as your dog's fur or a little longer.

🐾 DOG TOOTHBRUSH/TOOTHPASTE

Dental hygiene is EXTREMELY important for dogs. It is very important to start brushing your dog's teeth when he is a puppy, even though he will end up losing his puppy teeth.

Q *What kind of toothpaste should I get?*

First off, NEVER use human toothpaste when brushing your dog's teeth. Human toothpaste contains fluoride, which is **very** dangerous to dogs.

You can find dog-specific toothpaste (at any pet store) that usually comes with a two-sided toothbrush; refer to the "Brushing Teeth" part of Section 5 for more information on brushing your puppy's teeth.

🐾 Ear Cleaning Solution

Cleaning your pup's ears should be a very important part of your weekly routine in order to prevent ear infections.

You can buy ear-cleaning solution from any pet store. You will also need cotton balls and/or gauze along with the solution. Refer to the "Ear Cleaning" section of Section 5 for more information on cleaning your dog's ears.

🐾 Dog Shampoo

Dog fur is very different from human hair. **DO NOT use human shampoo** or any other kind of soap on your dog! Dog shampoo has been created to meet the specific needs of dogs' coats and skin.

Q *So what kind of shampoo should I get?*

There are so many different kinds of dog shampoos out there, many of which are composed of ingredients that are too harsh for some dogs' skin. I recommend using an all-natural puppy shampoo. A puppy's coat is different than what his adult coat will be, and puppy skin is very sensitive. Puppy shampoo is composed of ingredients that are extra gentle and designed specifically for a puppy's skin and fur.

My absolute favorite line of dog shampoo is called "Earthbath." It is an all-natural line of grooming products and is seriously AMAZING. They have a variety of different types of shampoos that fit every dog's needs. Their puppy shampoo smells SO good, as do the rest of their adult dog shampoos.

Some dogs have EXTRA sensitive skin and require a hypoallergenic shampoo. If your puppy's skin seems to be itchy or has bumps on it after using a normal shampoo, switch him to a hypoallergenic formula.

🐾 DOG NAIL TRIMMERS

It is **crucial** for your puppy's health that you trim his nails! If you do not want to trim your puppy's nails yourself, you have the option to get them trimmed by a groomer. If you do feel comfortable cutting them by yourself, refer to the "Nail Clipping" part of Section 5 for a more detailed explanation on how to do this.

When buying nail trimmers for your dog, there are two main options:

1. Scissors-style:

    • **These are the kind of nail trimmers that I recommend.**

    • They resemble scissors, except the blade is curved and indented.

    • There are a variety of different sizes of this type of nail trimmer, so it is VERY important that you buy the right size for your dog's nails.

2. Guillotine-style:

    • These trimmers have a circular opening where you place the dog's nail.

- When you squeeze the handles, a small blade cuts across the circular opening.

- This type does work well for small dogs or puppies, but once your dog's nails get thicker, it is a lot harder to use these trimmers to cut your dog's nails well.

With ANY nail trimmer, be sure to purchase the properly sized blade and handle for your particular dog. Nail trimmers that are too big or too small for a pup's nails will not trim them efficiently.

🐾 Poop Bags

Unless you have collected hundreds of plastic grocery bags, you can't forget to buy poop bags! Purchase ANY kind you want!

🐾 Treat Pouch/Carrier

As you will read later on in this book, I strongly recommend having an easy-to-grab item that you can carry your pup's treats in. There are specific "dog treat pouches" you can purchase, or a fanny pack will do the trick!

🐾 First Aid Supplies

I strongly suggest having some first aid supplies on hand for your puppy. Many different companies make dog first aid kits and you'll be able to find them in any pet store.

You can also refer to the "Basic Veterinary Knowledge" part of Section 5 for information on some of the supplies you might need. Make sure you are prepared!

❧ HEARTWORM, FLEA, AND TICK PREVENTATIVES

Yes, you absolutely **need** these preventatives. They can be costly, but they are also a simple measure you can take to prevent your pup from contracting a horrible disease.

Refer to the "Basic Veterinary Knowledge" part of Section 5 for more information on each of these preventatives individually.

❧ ITEMS I DON'T RECOMMEND PURCHASING

You may have noticed that I have not included Puppy Pads on this list. I don't recommend using them when house training your puppy because, honestly, it is a waste of time. You have to train your puppy to go potty on the Puppy Pads, just like you will have to teach him to go potty outside. So once you train your puppy to go on the pad, you end up having to train him to go outside anyway. It's a waste of time. **You don't decrease the chance of accidents in the house, and you double the work required!** Puppy Pads are an unnecessary extra step in the house training process that is not at all beneficial.

How To Prepare Your Living Space

Once again, it's up to you to decide where you want to place the crate. Much of it depends on where you have room for it in your home. However, choose wisely; **setting up the crate in the proper location is very important.** It is going to be your dogs's safe place the moment he gets to your home, and you need to ensure that he feels safe, regardless of where this location may be.

Q *What would be an ideal location?*

For the first week or so after bringing your new pup home, I recommend keeping the crate in your room.

Q *Why?*

As we'll discuss in the next step of raising the dog of your dreams, it's crucial that when introducing your new pup into your home you make him feel comfortable in his crate as soon as possible. Keeping your pup's crate in your room as he goes through this difficult transition will be imperative in helping him feel safer in his crate.

Not only will it make the crate training adjustment period easier, it will also work hand in hand with getting your pup potty trained as soon as possible. For instance, if your puppy is crying in the middle of the night because he has to go outside, you want to make sure that you can hear him. If you don't wake up and take your puppy out, you risk having him be forced to go to the bathroom in his crate, which will immensely backtrack the crate training and house training process. So, although he will be disrupting your beauty sleep, you want to wake up to your pup's signal that he needs to go potty while he develops good habits.

Q *Do I have to leave my puppy's crate in my room forever?*

Definitely not! Once your puppy is sleeping through the night on a consistent basis, you can move the crate if you want. I suggest putting it by the door you use to take him outside. That way it is easier to let him out and go directly outside to avoid an accident in the house.

> I also suggest placing a comfortable blanket or mat in the crate. Be very cautious that your puppy is not chewing it up, though. If he is, you will need to remove the bedding. You do not want your puppy eating a large piece of fabric or stuffing that could result in him needing surgery to remove it.

Q *Where should I put my puppy's toys?*

I suggest putting all of the puppy's toys in a container or bin. This will help teach the puppy which things are his toys. If you can, keep this bin next to the crate, as well as everything else that belongs to your pup.

Having a puppy corner in my house has kept things a lot easier and helped me separate my puppy's belongings from my own.

Q *I don't want my puppy having access to every room in the house. What should I do?*

The next step in preparing your house is to block off areas where you don't want your puppy to go. Whether that means just remembering to always close doors or putting up gates, it is important to utilize your control to set your pup's boundaries.

Q *Do I need a specific place where my puppy will go to the bathroom?*

Yes. Choose a designated area of your yard to be the puppy's potty area, and then bring him to that spot every time you go outside. You want to teach the puppy that this is the area for going to the bathroom. That doesn't mean the puppy can't go outside of the area, but it will be easier for him to associate "outside" with going potty if you always bring him to the same spot.

When To Bring Your Pup Home

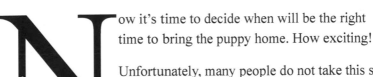

Now it's time to decide when will be the right time to bring the puppy home. How exciting!

Unfortunately, many people do not take this step into careful consideration because they are just so excited to bring the puppy home, so you need to be very careful with how you approach this.

Often I get asked the question, "I have everything ready Kaelin, when do I finally get to bring my puppy home?!"

My answer is… it depends! The main factor to take into account is the age of your dog. Whether your pup is 6 weeks old or 6 months old makes a big difference!

For instance, most rescues and breeders require your pup to be at least eight weeks old before releasing the pup to their new home.

So if you're about to burst at the seams with excitement but your pup is only 6 weeks old, you may REALLY want to jump the gun and just bring him home!

However, this is where you need to be incredibly patient.

Trust me, as a dog lover my entire life, I UNDERSTAND how it feels to be so elated about the thought of getting a new puppy that you just wish the day would come already!

However, try to shift your perspective for a few moments.

Imagine that YOU were the one being stripped away from your mother and siblings, and YOU were forced to move into a new home with strange creatures that made weird rules for you.

If you are bringing home a brand new puppy, this is most likely the first time the pup has been away from his mother and siblings, and it's going to be a whole different world for him!

But I'm not just trying to make you feel bad for your pup!

Not only is separating a pup from his litter too soon emotionally debilitating, but it is also damaging to their development into a confident and well-behaved pup as well.

This makes the 5-8 week period incredibly vital for a pup's development, being that this is when puppies learn how to socialize, how to control the intensity of their bite (through play with their littermates) and how to correctly interpret the body language of other dogs.

Pups placed in homes before going through this stage tend to develop more behavior problems, such as:

- Destructiveness
- Biting
- Excessive barking
- Reactivity and aggression
- Resource guarding
- Separation anxiety

While your eagerness to bring your new puppy home is harmless in its intent, the ramifications of your pup's lack of socialization due to early separation can cause a whole host of issues down the road.

Q *So, when is it okay to bring you puppy home?*

The rule of thumb is that puppies are ready go to their new homes in the 8-to-12 week old age range. If your pup is in that age range or older than that, then go for it!

If you're adopting an older dog, this is a different story.

With older dogs, the biggest thing to take into consideration is the dog's past and any negative experiences they have been through.

- *Has the dog been through a traumatic experience?*
- *Does the dog have any history of exhibiting behavioral issues?*
- *Does the dog play well with children, other dogs, and pets?*

These are just a few questions that you should take into consideration before bringing home an older dog. Lots of things can happen in a dog's life, and unfortunately, not every dog owner cares as much about their pup as you do! Be sure to chat with the rescue or previous owner to dive deep into the dog's past. When you do this, you'll see if you need to adjust the introduction process in any way (it's super important to be proactive and consult with a behaviorist in your area if you are concerned about creating tension in your household when adopting a new dog).

As we'll talk about in the next section, the first two weeks that the dog (whether a puppy or an older dog) is introduced into his new home is the most crucial time to ground his emotional psyche, create comfort, and establish good habits for your dog.

In fact, I strongly suggest making the sacrifice of taking time off or making sure you have a lot of extra time during this period to be able to help familiarize the pup with his new home, introduce a daily routine, and to start training immediately.

Bringing Your Puppy Home - Creating Comfort

🐾 WHAT TO EXPECT IN THE FIRST 72 HOURS

Remember, your puppy's whole life as he once knew it is now changing completely. **Every dog is different in how they will react to this change**, but I will address some common occurrences that may happen with your pup during the first few days.

Be prepared for sleepless nights.

Yes, puppies are just like babies. Your puppy will most likely cry and bark during the first few nights (or longer) until he is fully crate trained:

- Because he doesn't like being confined in the crate.
- Because he misses his family.
- BOTH.

These reasons aside, if your puppy falls asleep and then wakes up in the middle of the night crying or barking, he most likely needs to go outside to go potty. Keep in mind that depending on the age of your pup, for the first few weeks or so you may have to get up once or twice in the middle of the night to take your puppy out. Don't worry; this doesn't last too long as long as you follow my crate training advice! Your pup will learn to hold it through the night fairly quickly.

Q *Do all puppies have accidents in the house?*

I can almost *guarantee* you that your puppy will have accidents. Even older dogs that are house trained sometimes have accidents in new places because they aren't sure where they are supposed to go. Your puppy WILL have accidents, so be prepared for this and do not get upset when it happens. Refer to the house training section in Section 3 for more information on what to do when your puppy has an accident.

KEYS TO SUCCESS

If you're a first time puppy owner, be prepared for possible sleepless nights, accidents in the house, and crying. This is completely normal for the puppy's first several nights while he's getting acclimated to his new environment.

How And When To Feed Your Pup

Q *Where and when should I feed my pup?*

Feedings should ALWAYS take place in the crate. I highly advise you to do this because:

1. Most puppies are food motivated and feeding in the crate is extremely important in getting your puppy acclimated to the crate.

2. To allow his food to digest.

   To avoid any digestion issues, puppies should rest immediately after eating. If a puppy is allowed freedom to play and run, he will certainly take advantage of that.

Q *Should I feed my puppy a certain amount? Or should I free feed him?*

DO NOT free feed your puppy. Some say you should free feed your puppy so he "gets as much food as he needs." This advice is detrimental to your pup's health and your ability to effectively train your puppy.

Q *Why?*

The simple answer is that free feeding isn't beneficial for your puppy or you in establishing a routine. Here are five reasons why you shouldn't free feed your pup:

1. **It can put your puppy at risk of becoming overweight.** Many puppies have eyes that are larger than their stomachs. When Juneau was a puppy, I swear she would have eaten the whole bag in one meal if I'd let her!

2. **When food is always available in the crate, it makes the food and the crate much less appealing.** If something is always available for you, you won't wish to have it as often. The same goes for dogs!

   You want your puppy to get excited for mealtime and get excited to go into the crate to eat.

3. **It is important to keep track of how much you are feeding your puppy at each meal** to ensure he is getting enough to meet his nutritional needs.

   For people serious about their puppy's health, free feeding makes things a lot more stressful and unorganized because you aren't able to monitor how much your puppy is eating. If you end up having to cut down on your puppy's food intake for some health reason, how will you know how much your puppy has to be fed now when you are free feeding him? When you are free feeding, measurement is impossible.

4. **It will lead to more accidents in the house.**

. Why? Well think about it— when you have routine, timely feeds, you know that you can expect your puppy to have to poop about 30 minutes to an hour after eating. However, if your puppy is constantly eating while being free fed, you will not know when exactly he needs to go out, which will lead to more accidents in the house due to an irregular feeding schedule.

5. **It sacrifices your ability to monitor your puppy's healthy habits.**

When a puppy is not eating, it should be a red flag to you; **loss of appetite is one of the best indicators of illness in dogs.** Therefore, when you are free feeding your puppy, you can't really tell if your puppy skipped lunch that day or not. Your puppy needs to have balanced meals that are appropriately portioned to stay healthy and happy, another reason why I am against free feeding.

Q *If I can't free feed my pup, how do I know how much to feed him?*

By following your vet's portion size recommendations, your dog will get enough food eating just three times a day. Obviously, it won't always be exact, but **aim to feed your puppy every four to six hours, three times per day.** If you haven't yet taken your pup to the vet, follow the portion size guidelines identified by weight on the puppy food label until you can double check it with your vet.

BRIGHT IDEAS

Start off right with your puppy by establishing proper training habits such as ALWAYS crate feeding your pup on a strict schedule — according to your vet's portion recommendations. This will make the house training process quicker and lessen the chance of your pup having accidents inside.

Q *What if my pup won't eat his meal when he's in the crate?*

If your puppy is not food motivated when his meal is in front of him in the crate, you've got to *make* him become food motivated.

How?

You may be skeptical at first to think that you could make your puppy like food more, but it's a lot easier than you think:

- Leave food in the crate for only 10-15 minutes.
- Take the bowl out after 10-15 minutes no matter how much he has eaten.
- *Do not* offer him food again until the next meal

Owners often tell me that they would feel bad taking the food away and not offering it again until the next meal time, but you have to get over this guilt. A puppy is not going to starve himself if there is food sitting right in front of him!

This limited-time feeding approach teaches the puppy that mealtime is when Mom/Dad says it's mealtime and he needs to eat now if he wants to have lunch!

The First Day: Acclimating Your Pup

·········· 🐾 ··········

Finally being able to bring your new puppy home is SO exciting! However, the first couple days can also be the most stressful. You have to remember that change is hard on dogs and can be very stressful for them. Remember, your puppy's life is completely changing. **If this is your pup's first time being away from his mother and/or siblings, it can be especially difficult on him.** Luckily, dogs adapt to change a lot faster than humans do. By following these guidelines, you can make the process of bringing your pup home and introducing him to his new life a lot smoother.

🐾 CHECK THE ESSENTIALS

Make sure to find out what your pup has done that day prior to bringing him home. Here is a basic checklist of what you should do immediately upon bringing your puppy home:

🐾 Depending on what time of the day you bring the puppy home, find out the last time he ate and when he was last outside to go potty.

🐾 **Before** bringing your puppy inside, take him to the designated potty area outside and wait for five minutes to see if he will go potty.

🐾 When you bring your puppy into the house, show him the puppy corner and familiarize him with the crate.

KEYS TO SUCCESS

Use this checklist and the suggestions in this section to properly familiarize your pup with his new home and help the two of you start off on the right paw!

Q *When should I start training my pup?*

It is important to start training the puppy on good behaviors immediately. Even if it's only for a few minutes, try to put the puppy in his crate with a chew toy or food (if it is meal time) as soon as possible. If your pup is not interested, try other chewing objects or treats until he likes something enough that he will interact with it for several minutes. If done correctly, your pup will immediately associate the crate and your home in general with positivity; now you're off to a great start!

I always stress the importance of education before commitment with dog owners to ensure that they truly know what they're getting into with their dog. While it's true that any dog is trainable, it would be naive to think that every dog is the same to train. How you train your dog from this point forward will of course play an integral part in how well-behaved and trained your dog ends up being. It's also imperative to be realistic and practical about how genetics and your dog's past may impact future results. An abused rescue dog with aggression is going to be *much* more difficult to train than an eight week old Labrador Retriever with no history of abuse.

Understanding Your Dog

Every single dog is different. I stress this concept so much because it is important to realize that your pup is so much different than the puppy next door. **There are no "secrets" or "hacks" that will make every single dog listen to you, and there is not a single reward that appeals to every single dog.** A dog's uniqueness makes each one of them very different to train, and their behaviors stem from two things: genetics and environment. Simply put, dogs are born with certain behavioral traits based on their breed and then become a product of their environment based on how they are raised and trained.

However, when looking at the science and behavioral history of most dog breeds, you'll find that the relationship is much more complex. While your pup's genetics may predispose him to behave in certain ways, genetics are only a single piece of the puzzle. Behavior develops through a complex interaction between environment and genetics. This is an especially important consideration when analyzing an individual pup compared to his breed. A number of diverse and often subtle factors influence the development of behavior, including, but not limited to, nutrition, stress on the mother during pregnancy and even womb temperature during development. And when it comes to influencing and developing the behaviors of your unique pup, elements such as the environment in which he was raised and his history of social interactions play key roles in behavioral development. The plethora of elements that feed into the expression of your pup's behavioral tendencies are so intricately intertwined that it's usually impossible to pinpoint any one specific factor that accounts for certain behavioral traits.

The reason I'm telling you this is because the different behaviors that are the result of **genetics will likely have a HUGE influence on how YOUR pup will respond to training**. This is why I recommend in Section 1 to research your pup's breed before making an adoption decision. For example, Huskies are an incredibly stubborn breed and don't necessarily care to please their owners. Golden Retrievers, on the other hand, are family dogs and *really* seek to please. Thus, Golden Retrievers typically are easier to train because it is in their genetics and bloodline to want to listen to their owners and make them happy.

However, keep in mind that just because your puppy's breed typically possesses certain behavioral traits due to his genetics, that doesn't mean that your puppy will exhibit these behaviors. And even if he does, every behavior can be reworked with thorough training! As I explained earlier, there's much more involved in behavioral development than just breed disposition; it's crucial to be aware of factors other than just genetics that may impact your pup's behavioral tendencies.

While you pup's genetics and past experiences are out of your control, your puppy's current living situation will still play a pivotal part in shaping him into a happy, healthy and well-trained member of your family, which is completely within your control. This is why I stressed such an extensive puppy preparation process in the first Section of this book. Going through all the necessary steps will put you in the best position to shape your pup into the best dog possible!

Following my guidelines will help to create an environment that is the best for your puppy, but **your energy and actions will also have a great influence on your dog's behavior.** I am happy to guide you every step of the way, but ultimately, it comes down to YOU executing on these principles in order to become the best puppy parent possible.

KEYS TO SUCCESS

Remember that your puppy is a unique individual and will respond to training at his own pace. There are no secrets that will make every single dog listen to you and there is not a single reward that appeals to every single dog. Keep this practical tip in mind as you continue your puppy parenthood journey.

🐾 RECOGNIZING STRESS SIGNALS

To be able to better understand your puppy, you need to understand his body language and behaviors. When dogs are feeling stressed or uncomfortable in a situation, they <u>will</u> warn you. Unfortunately, many dog owners fail to recognize that these behavioral signals are warnings signs of stress.

It's very important to recognize these behaviors as warnings and to remove your dog from the situation. If nothing is done after your dog signals that he is uncomfortable or stressed, his behavior could turn into aggression, so you want to make sure this outcome is prevented. Keep in mind that every pup is different in the warning signals he uses when stressed, so watch for any of the following:

🐕 **Stress yawning**

- This is different than a tired yawn in that it is done more intensely and often times repeatedly.

🐕 **Licking of lips**

- This is different than a dog licking his lips because food is around.

🐕 **Pinning ears back**

- His ears will lay down and point behind him.

🐕 Avoidance

- Turning his head away or attempting to move away.

🐕 Excessive panting

- Panting excessively not because he is tired or hot could mean he is stressed.

🐕 Growling

- Growling is a straightforward indicator that your dog is uncomfortable.

🐕 Low-positioned tail

- Tail is out low or between legs, often times only the end is wagging.

🐕 Dog is suddenly biting at his own paws

- He is doing this out of nowhere, for no reason other than he is uncomfortable in the situation that he is in.

If you have ever noticed one of these stress signals in your dog, take a few minutes here to think about what made your dog uncomfortable in that particular situation.

Did he see another dog?

Did he hear an unusual or loud noise?

Did a stranger try to approach him?

Take the time to understand and be aware of your dog's stress signals. Once you are aware, then you will be able to use the principles in this book to properly desensitize your dog of the stressful stimuli.

Also, it is immensely important to NEVER scold your puppy for exhibiting these warning behaviors, even growling. If you scold him for showing warnings, he may just skip the warning step and go straight into being aggressive so please consult a behaviorist before trying anything rash.

BRIGHT IDEAS

Use this list to identify your dog's personal stress signals so that you can learn to recognize them and accordingly remove him from stressful situations.

How To Train Your Dog — Teaching Your Puppy To Listen To And Respect Your Commands

❧

MY 5 "GOLDEN RULES" OF DOG TRAINING

Whenever I talk about my "Golden Rules" of dog training to my clients, people are amazed at just how simple yet effective these principles are! While some of these principles may seem like common sense to some, they are completely new to others. Regardless of where you're starting, I promise that when you consistently apply these principles along with the tools I'm giving you throughout the rest of this book, the results you will see are absolutely incredible in terms of getting your dog to listen to you and develop a solid foundation of obedience.

Positive Reinforcement Is EVERYTHING

Positive reinforcement training is all about REWARDING your dog for the behaviors that you DO want him to repeat. Rewards can be treats, affection, toys, or anything else he loves and will associate as a positive thing. This concept sounds simple, but is often actually overlooked.

On this same note, don't disregard when your dog IS behaving for you. After telling my clients this, I often hear responses along the lines of: "I never overlook when Fluffy is behaving—he gets so much attention all the time!", to which I respond with, "Great!"

Meanwhile, the puppy is chewing on his chew toy and being completely ignored... Yet the second the puppy starts chewing on the couch, the owner is very quick to tell the puppy he is doing the wrong thing.

Q *What's wrong with this?*

Whenever your pup is sitting calmly, focusing on you, or behaving like you want him to always behave, remember to REWARD him! More emphasis should be put on making a BIG deal out of the desirable behavior than directing all of your negative attention and frustration into the issues.

> The more you reinforce that you desire these behaviors and reward your dog for exhibiting them, the more he will choose to exhibit these wanted behaviors.

Understanding and living by this basic principle is absolutely imperative for you to train the best dog possible!

ALWAYS ASSOCIATE YOUR DOG'S NAME WITH POSITIVITY

Always say your dog's name positively! Never in a scolding tone. Any time your dog responds to you saying his name, even if it's just simply looking at you or coming to you, tell him "YES" and reward him. This way, your pup will begin to learn early on that hearing his name is a positive experience that is typically followed by a reward (whether that is a treat, toy, or simply their owner's love and affection).

Establishing that you calling your dog's name as a positive thing is the first major step to establishing strong recall habits.

Later on, when your dog is off leash and he starts to run after another dog, you are going to call him to come by his name:

"Rover, come!"

If, however, your pup's name is used in a scolding tone, he is going to look at you and think: "Am I in trouble, or am I getting a reward? Ehhh, I'm not going to chance it!" *Dog then bolts off towards another dog*

NEVER REPEAT A COMMAND MORE THAN ONCE

Whenever you are commanding your dog to do something, only say the command ONE TIME. When properly enforced, this teaches your pup that he needs to perform the command immediately after being commanded only once, so that you don't get in the habit of telling your pup to "sit" twenty times before he actually sits.

If, however, your dog doesn't perform the command right away after you say it:

- Reinforce the hand gesture you're using for the particular command.

- Say your dog's name, a "kissy" sound, or any other sound to refocus his attention back to you and the hand gesture.

- Be patient, do not repeat the command, and he WILL perform the wanted command!

- When your dog performs what you are asking him to do, be sure to tell him "YES" immediately and reward him!

- Always follow through with what you ask your dog to do and be consistent!

If your pup is too distracted or not listening to the command after you have tried the above instructions, do whatever it takes to get him to listen to you (find something more motivating, lure him to you with a treat, leash him, etc). Whatever you choose, be sure that you do not give up so that your dog knows that he needs to listen to you every single time — no exceptions!

REDIRECTION IS KEY TO SHAPING BEHAVIOR

Whenever your furry friend is chewing on an unwanted object, tell him "NO" and redirect him to an object that he IS allowed to chew on. When you see him exhibiting that annoying behavior, redirecting him to something else will be key to helping him understand what *is* and *is not* appropriate behavior. If, however, you only tell your pup "NO", and give him no object of redirection, your pup will likely get confused and continue to perform the same behaviors which you are attempting to change.

> In essence, you want to give your pup motivation to stop doing what he is doing, so you need to give him something else to do instead.

Whether this be redirecting your dog to play with a toy, a bone to chew on, or making his mind work by telling him to sit or lay down, you as the dog owner need to reverse engineer WHY your pup is chewing on the couch (because he possesses an instinctual need to chew), and help divert his instinctual tendencies into a healthy outlet, such as chewing on a toy or other appropriate chewing object.

TRAINING SHOULD BE FUN!

Training is tough, but it's also FUN! To make this process less intimidating, you really need to have a good time with training—make it fun for both you and your pup. **It will go much more smoothly and efficiently if you go into it with a positive attitude!** Make training a fun and happy thing so that your puppy will get excited about it and look forward to it! Just remember that puppies have short attention spans, so do not get frustrated when your pup starts checking out. There is a reason I only offer my clients one-hour long training sessions: dogs do not typically have attention spans any longer than that!

The TRUTH About How Long It Takes To Train Your Pup

With the rise of the internet and easy access to (untrustworthy) information outlets around the world, dog training has become one of the most misunderstood areas in animal behaviorism. Since it's also the most popular field of animal behaviorism, it comes as no surprise that EVERYONE has their opinion when it comes to the "best" way to train your dog.

This is a dangerous truth because with the power of the internet and the ease with which content spreads, any well-designed blog can begin sending out misguided information about dogs and dog training; often misinforming hundreds or even thousands of people in the process. All that misinformation creates a number of myths that dog-training posers like to use in their programs. One of such myths is "how long" it takes to train a puppy.

BRIGHT IDEAS

Be VERY careful who you take dog training advice from. EVERYONE has their own opinion when it comes to the "best" way to train your dog, and much of it is misleading. Guard your thoughts and allow yourself to be skeptical of dog resources that make bold claims without evidence.

Q *How long will it take to train my puppy?*

People ask me ALL the time, "How long will it take to train my puppy?" I hate to break it to you, but there is no right answer to this question. However, I understand where questions like this come from. Dog training marketers are CONSTANTLY bombarding dog owners with misleading claims that they can train your puppy in "X amount of days." I would be weary of such programs, because as a dog trainer with over a decade of experience, I can confidently say that every single dog I've trained has been different in some way. There is no one-size-fits-all approach, and there certainly isn't a single time frame that applies to all dogs.

Seriously, how can anyone claim to be able to train your dog in a certain number of days? Every single dog learns at his own speed! Some are faster learners than others. Some puppies exhibit behaviors due to their genetics and past experiences that make training more difficult, while others have traits and experiences that make training easier. And even then, not every dog of the same breed is going to have identical behaviors and intelligence.

Every single dog has his own personality, intelligence level, and overall behavior. There are a plethora of possible genetic and environmental factors that can lead your pup to be more or less receptive to training, which makes training guarantees like this absurd.

Q *What do you consider a 'trained' dog?*

I find that many people have different definitions of what a "trained" dog actually means to them.

What do YOU consider to be a trained dog? Just having a dog that sits on command every time? Or do you envision having a dog that listens to you every time, is crate and house trained, and knows all kinds of tricks? Refer back to 'How to Successfully Use This Book' to help you identify exactly what your goals are in training your puppy. Your answers will assist you in the training process by giving you a more focused game plan.

Although I cannot guarantee that your pup will be trained in "X amount of days," **I CAN guarantee that by thoroughly following my guidelines throughout this book, and busting your butt, your dog will be trained in the fastest way he can possibly be trained.** Whether that's three weeks, three months or three years, the time it takes to train your dog depends on your dog as an individual and how much time and effort YOU as his owner are willing to invest into the training process.

KEYS TO SUCCESS

NEVER put a time limit on how long it should take
to train your new pup. Remember that every dog is
unique and possesses a unique makeup depending
on their genetics and environment. Keep this in the back
of your mind as you begin training your pup. If you get
frustrated, return to patience and positivity.

Introduction To Training

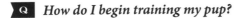

Q *How do I begin training my pup?*

Since the beginning stages of the positive reinforcement training process involves using treats to reward your puppy for good behavior, it is pivotal for you to find a treat that your puppy truly loves. If your dog is very food motivated like most puppies, it will make training much easier. However, if your puppy is not food motivated, don't get discouraged! Explore and find something that your puppy absolutely LOVES.

When I was training Juneau, she was such a little piglet and would eat almost anything, so I just used her puppy kibble as treats and she loved it! Grizzly on the other hand, is food motivated only when other dogs are food motivated, he just goes along with anything they are doing. If they are getting super excited about treats, he will get super excited about the treats. If they aren't there, he doesn't seem to care very much and isn't as food motivated. This goes to show that **every** dog is truly different in how they behave, and you MUST be able to adapt to these differences.

Q *What kind of treats do you recommend?*

If you skipped past The Puppy Preparation Checklist, I will restate that I usually recommend Sojo's 100% Raw Freeze-Dried treats. Dogs LOVE them and they are very nutritious. You want very, very small treats so you don't give your puppy too much at once. I split the treats into tiny pieces when I am doing an hour-long training session in order to minimize treat intake and keep the dog motivated.

Any kind of soft treats will work much better for training than hard ones. I recommend any soft treats that have limited ingredients. They're healthier and are typically low in calorie content, so that you can give your dog more without upsetting his stomach.

Keep in mind that you should always be reading the ingredient labels on dog treats/food so that you know exactly what you are feeding your dog!

Q **"If I use treats as motivation for training, will my dog end up only listening to me when I am holding a treat?"**

This is a great question, and one that I get often. Many dog owners message me with questions regarding training and tell me that their dog only listens to them when they are holding a treat. Typically this behavior also stems from other factors that can be avoided by following my Golden Rules Of Training from the start. Some dogs are, however, incredibly stubborn unless the owner is holding up the reward of a treat. The reason for this is usually because the dog was trained using treats, and then the owner stopped using treats cold-turkey, which is a *big* mistake. If your place of employment all of the sudden told you that you will no longer be paid for your work, would you be motivated to do your job? I don't think so!

To avoid this issue, we will evolve through different stages of training to wean off of the treats in a way that will result in your dog holding the same focus on you whether there is a treat in your hand or not.

🐾 USING A "CLICKER WORD"

You probably have seen people at the pet store training classes using a clicker to train their dog. If you don't know what I'm talking about, a clicker is a little plastic device that makes a clicking noise when you push down on the button. When training your dog, you are supposed to make the clicking noise when he exhibits the correct behavior and pair it with a treat. Then your puppy associates the clicking noise with a reward. **I do believe that the clicker method works, but are you going to keep a clicker on you at all times? 24/7?**

Instead of using a physical clicker device, I like to use a "clicker" that I am forced to have on me at all times: my voice. For training purposes, choose a simple clicker word that you will use to signal to your pup that he has correctly done what you are asking him to do.

NOTE: I say a specific word instead of phrase because you want something very short and sweet.

KEYS TO SUCCESS

One of the biggest myths surrounding dog training is that you need a clicker to effectively train your pup. Instead of relying on a clicker device, harness the power of your voice to command your pup as his pack leader.

Q *Can I say "good boy" or "good girl"?*

A lot of people ask if they can use "good boy" or "good girl" as their clicker word. I say **no** for two reasons:

1. You want a one-syllable word that is easy to use and fast to say.

2. You want to choose a word that you don't say all the time.

How often do you tell your pup that he's such a good boy? My guess is a LOT, probably more often than you even realize. Instead, you want a word that is easily distinguished by your puppy as the clicker word and that he knows means: "I did exactly what Mom/Dad asked me to do."

Q *What do you suggest using instead?*

Personally, I use the word "yes" as my clicker word when training dogs; it has been incredibly successful in my training experiences, and dogs respond very well to it. Why? It is easy, fast, and I don't find myself just telling my dog "yes" unless we are working on training. Therefore, my dogs are less likely to confuse it with other words, which makes "yes" the PERFECT clicker word for me. Other examples of clicker words you might want to use are "good" and "right."

BRIGHT IDEAS

When choosing the best clicker word for your situation, be sure to choose a one-syllable word that can be easily and quickly distinguished by your pup.

Q *How do I use a clicker word?*

As we will discuss next in the 5 stages of training a new command, the early stages of training a new command involve the clicker word being followed by a treat or other reward such as physical affection. In your dog's mind: 'clicker word' + treat = I did exactly what was asked of me!

KEYS TO SUCCESS

Always follow your clicker word with a treat or reward for your dog. This will teach him that he gets a reward when he follows your commands. 'Clicker word' + treat = reward for your pup.

Q *Why is a clicker word necessary?*

I am a firm believer in using treats, treats, and more treats as a means of motivating the dog during the early stages of training. But when it comes time to wean off of the treats as your pup's reward, the clicker word will become your most important tool. Using the clicker word to wean your pup off treat training ensures that your dog will keep intense focus on you whether you are holding a treat in your hand or not. The clicker word is also very beneficial when you do not have treats on you but want to tell your dog he did the right thing.

Often I see this scenario:

An owner tells their dog to come. The dog comes. The owner tells the dog to sit. The dog sits. The owner tells the dog to lay down. The dog lays down. The owner then walks away...

The dog is then left thinking: "I did all three things that were asked of me, right?! Did I not do something right?"

Dogs need to be told when they do the right thing every time so that they are motivated to do it the next time you ask. Dogs, forever, want to please you and thrive off of your praise. If you just walk away from your dog after he performs a command, without giving any praise or reward, why would he want to do it again? This is especially crucial for puppies, who are just learning what is right and what is not. **You must tell a puppy when he is doing the right thing. Otherwise, he has no idea that it is right.**

🐾 THE 5 STAGES OF TRAINING A NEW COMMAND

················ (1) ················

SHOW HAND GESTURE AND LURE PUP - REWARD WITH CLICKER WORD AND TREAT.

During the beginning of training, your dog is obviously still learning and trying to understand the commands that you are trying to teach him. The basic process is as follows:

- Give the hand gesture for the command you are trying to teach.

- Say the verbal command.

- Lure the dog to the position you are commanding him to go to.

- Reward with a treat and clicker word every single time he correctly performs the command.

SHOW HAND GESTURE - REWARD WITH CLICKER WORD AND TREAT.

Once the dog is making the connection between the verbal command and/or hand gesture and his body positioning, you can cut out the luring. This takes a little patience on your end. Give the hand gesture and verbal command and wait a few seconds to see if it will click for your pup without luring. As with every aspect of training, you will be surprised what your pup will accomplish with just a little patience from you!

SHOW HAND GESTURE - REWARD WITH CLICKER WORD AND A TREAT EVERY OTHER TIME.

Once your dog performs a command immediately every time you command him (verbally and with the hand gesture), you will want to reward him with the clicker word, but slowly start to wean off of the treats and only reward him with a treat every other command.

> *** BEGINNER MISTAKE:** A lot of people wean off of treats TOO FAST, so if you aren't sure if your dog is ready for this step yet, it is better to continue to reward with treats for a longer period of time than to nix the treats too fast.

SHOW HAND GESTURE - REWARD WITH CLICKER WORD AND "TRICKING" WITH TREATS

This step is important in making sure that your dog listens to YOU, rather than only listening for the treat. No matter if you are holding a treat up or not, we want your dog to be motivated by pleasing you!

To do this, you are essentially going to present the treat as usual and once he performs the command, you will reward him with only praise and the clicker word. You will also do this vice versa—command your pup to perform a command just by holding up the hand gesture and then once he executes the command, a treat will come out of nowhere (from your pocket).

This will keep your pup guessing about when he will actually be getting a treat, and by default, will also help him to transition into being motivated without a treat in his face.

SHOW HAND GESTURE — REWARD WITH CLICKER WORD AND OCCASIONAL TREATS

Once you consistently have your dog listening to your every command every single time, you have mastered the hardest part of training! For the future, you want to always use your clicker word, but treats should be used sparingly, if at all.

Training Protocol 101: What You NEED To Know

················ 🐾 ················

BEFORE I go into detail about specific commands that you will be teaching your pup, it is crucial that you understand the basic yet incredibly effective strategies that master obedience trainers and behaviorists use to generate exceptional results.

Q *How do I start training my dog?*

To first start training your pup, **start at home where he'll be familiar with his surroundings.** Follow the guideline below to assist you as you traverse this new and exciting process! Here are the most valuable training tips to remember as you begin training your pup:

🐕 Start training your pup in a quiet and secluded area of your home to gain as much of his attention as you can on you.

- Why? Immediately putting your puppy into a new setting outside of your home to train him will distract him. He will be more interested in this new area than whatever you're trying to teach him.

- I see this scenario all the time: A dog owner tells me that his dog does not listen to him when they are at the park (or any other distracting environment). So I first start with a training session at their home to go over the training basics, and see that the dog does not even listen to his owner in the home! If you can't hold your pup's attention in the most familiar, least-distracting environment possible, how can you expect to hold your pup's attention in a highly stimulating and extremely distracting environment?

🐕 While you should initially begin training your pup in familiar surroundings, DON'T limit your dog's training sessions to only familiar surroundings as he advances. Once your puppy gets past the beginning stages of training, be sure to include some distractions and new settings while training.

- **You want your dog to be focused and listening to you no matter where you may be.** If you only work on training your pup at home, maintaining his obedience in public will be an uphill battle as he grows older.

🐕 When training your pup, only say the command ONE time! (This is very important.)

- In fact, for the rest of your dog's life, you should only state the command you want to enforce ONCE.

  ★ This is the most common error people make when training their dog!

- For example, if you are trying to get your puppy to sit, you should NEVER say the command "sit" more than one time!

- If the pup doesn't sit after saying the command once, many people keep saying it until the puppy sits. This is a terrible mistake!

  * A lot of times people don't realize how many times they are really saying the command, as it is only natural to keep telling your dog what to do until he does it. If this describes you, work on being more self-aware of your energy and actions during training.

KEYS TO SUCCESS

Important training tips to remember as you begin training your pup:

1. Start training your pup in a quiet and private area of your home.
2. Include some distractions and new settings as your pup becomes more well-trained.
3. When training your dog, only issue a command ONE time! (VERY IMPORTANT)

Q *Why does it matter how many times I tell my puppy a command, as long as he does it?*

This is a VITAL point to understand very quickly in order to earn respect and obedience. **One of the largest hurdles you must overcome in training your pup is making him understand that YOU are the pack leader, not him, and he NEEDS to listen to you.** Therefore, you want your puppy to learn to listen to you after you say something only once. If you say "sit" three times before your puppy finally sits, this will teach him that he doesn't have to do what you ask until you tell him three times; or even worse, some dogs will test you to see how many times you will say a command before just giving up. It may seem malicious, but it's not, it's simply a resistance of control.

Q *What am I supposed to do if my puppy isn't listening after I say a command once?*

- In order to teach your dog the self-control you so deeply desire, you must be aware of yourself and your actions during training as well. Make it a practice to only say a command once and use a training partner/friend to keep both of you accountable to this Golden Rule.

- Continue to reinforce the hand gesture (which you will read later in this section) and maintain your pup's attention.

- If his attention strays, regain it.

- Put the treat back in front of his nose to remind him what he is working for.

- Although you won't state the command again, you can say your puppy's name or make any noise to try to get his focus back on you.

- If you watch my videos on social media, you'll find that I like to use the "kissy noise" a lot to get a dog's attention.

- Most dogs respond very well to this, and if you start using it right away while training, then it will catch on as a means to grab your dogs's attention.

A well-trained pup will exhibit the correct behavior after you command him just one time, as long as you are persistent with these tactics from the very beginning of training.

BRIGHT IDEAS

Use the "kissy noise" or another sound of your choice to regain your pup's attention. Use this instead of repeating the command you are trying to teach.

Q *How much should I practice training my puppy? Are there a certain number of repetitions that you recommend?*

This is a difficult question because every pup is different, and so are people's training goals. However, I DO recommend consistency in training and **working on a little a lot, rather than a lot a little.** What I mean by this is that it's better to deliberately practice a few skills with your puppy for a few minutes every day rather than over-whelming him with everything in this book once a week.

Think of it this way: is it more enjoyable for you to learn a difficult skill once a week for several hours straight? Or for ten minutes a day, every day? Obviously the second one! Dogs are very similar to humans in that they perform better at higher levels when mentally taxing, skill-building activities are spread out into shorter increments of focused practice rather than jammed into one, longer practice period. When following the first option, dogs (and their owners) tend to get impatient and lose focus. With that being said, trust your better judgment when it comes to scheduling training time and repetitions for your puppy. **Don't force your dog to train when he is clearly checked out** — this will not get you anywhere with training him and will only make him dislike training.

Q *How many people should be allowed to train my pup?*

Puppies are much like children in the sense that they will try to test you and see what they can get away with. They will do this with each person who cares for them, so it is important to have a strict set of guidelines that EVERYONE follows. While I don't set a rule for a pup only being trained by one person, I DO stress the importance of everyone enforcing the same guidelines.

🐾 KEEPING YOUR COOL: PROJECTING THE RIGHT EMOTIONS ON YOUR PUP

If at ANY time you or your puppy is getting frustrated, take a break! It can get discouraging if your puppy isn't catching on to something you are trying to train him to do. If this happens, your puppy WILL sense your frustrated energy, and it will only make training harder for both of you.

KEYS TO SUCCESS

Staying positive throughout the training process is incredibly important! Although it's easy to get frustrated when your pup isn't responding as you'd hoped, projecting negative emotions will only make him dislike training and hurt his progress.

Take a little break or move on to the next exercise. Don't force your dog to do anything he does not want to do. Never push your pup into the position you want him to take. Don't get upset if your pup doesn't catch onto a trick the first time you introduce it or even the second or third time. You are building a lifelong relationship of trust and respect; allow for an ample amount of time to build such a bond. Perfection is impossible and issues are inevitable.

Remember, every dog is different, and it will take each puppy a different amount of time to thoroughly learn a trick or command!

Again, the most important thing you can do is be calm, cool, collected and consistent. Focus only on the things you can control! Meticulously follow my instructions for each training exercise, and I PROMISE your pup will end up learning each and every one!

Crate Training Your Pup

One of the biggest mistakes you can make when training your puppy is NOT crate training him. I PROMISE it will make both you and your puppy's lives SO much better. It does take some patience in the beginning, but after that, you will be at ease knowing that your dog is not only trained to be in his crate but enjoys being in it. As I mentioned before, dogs are den animals just like wolves—from which they derive. Therefore, dogs NEED their own space to feel safe and comfortable.

It is *not* cruel.

It is *not* a punishment.

It is *not* inhumane.

By crate training your dog you are giving him the safe space that his ancestors have evolved to depend on. Anybody who tells you that a dog should never be crated or that it's animal abuse simply is not educated on the subject.

> ### KEYS TO SUCCESS
>
> Crate training your pup is a pivotal step in the training process that should NOT be skipped!

However, keep in mind that your puppy will most likely NOT like his crate at first. He will bark, yell, howl, whine, etc. This can be extremely frustrating for you (especially when it's your bed time) but **DO NOT give in and let the puppy out!** The number one rule for crate training is to NOT let the puppy out of the crate when he is making noise—whether it be whining, barking, howling, or any sound or behavior you do not want him to be making. You may think that this is the best way to get the puppy to settle and quiet down, but you will only be making it harder on yourself and the puppy in the long run by giving into this self-rewarding behavior.

Why?

When a dog is crying because he doesn't want to be inside of the crate, letting him out teaches him that when he cries, he gets his way! Then, the puppy associates crying with him getting what he wants, and then guess what comes next: he will begin to cry whenever he wants something! This is obviously not a behavior you want your puppy to continue doing! Think of it like this: When your child is throwing a tantrum because he wants to go outside and play instead of first cleaning up his toys, would you give him what he wants just because he is crying? If so, your child is going to think that whenever he throws a tantrum, you are going to end up giving in and he will not have to follow through on appropriate behavior.

Q *Do all dogs cry when first exposed to the crate?*

Every dog will respond differently to the crate depending on his or her prior exposure to crate training and overall behavioral disposition. The person who previously cared for your dog may have already started crate training, or the puppy may never have even seen a crate before. There is always the unfortunate chance—especially if he or she was rescued and you don't know his prior history—that your puppy was exposed to the crate in a negative way. If this is the case, you will have to approach crate training very slowly and cautiously.

Q *So how do I make my pup like being in his crate?*

First off, ALWAYS associate positivity with the crate, and NEVER use it as a form of punishment. Trust me, I know the temptation of wanting to put your dog in the crate to punish him when you are upset that he chewed up your shoes. This, however, will only cause the puppy to associate the crate with punishment and negativity. I'll say it again since it's so important: **the crate must be associated with ONLY POSITIVE THINGS.**

Q *So what are positive things?*

Since almost every healthy puppy is food-motivated, **dog food will be the most important positive tool to associate with the crate.** Feedings should always take place in the crate. Early on, when Juneau was a puppy and saw me filling her food bowl, she immediately ran into her crate and patiently waited for me to bring her food there. It doesn't take puppies long to pick up this behavior if you consistently feed them in the crate.

Other items you can use to associate the crate positively would include all of the **chewing objects** discussed in the Puppy Preparation Checklist. I always have at least one or two chewing objects in the crate at all times. **Treats** are also a positive thing to give to your puppy when he is in the crate. However, don't ever leave a stuffed animal or any other toy that the puppy could destroy in the crate. You don't want to run the risk that he'll rip open the toy and ingest plastic or stuffing while you're gone.

> ### BRIGHT IDEAS
>
> ALWAYS associate your dog's crate with positivity in order to make the crate his 'safe place' that he enjoys being in. Doing this the right way decreases the chances of your puppy developing behavioral problems related to being in his crate.

Q *How much time should my pup spend in the crate?*

I get asked this question all the time, and while the answer can't be measured in a concrete number of hours, I will tell you this: **A puppy's entire day should revolve around the crate.** If you follow that advice alone, the whole puppy training process will be five million times easier, seriously.

However, the problem is that most owners make the mistake of revolving a puppy's day around being *out* of the crate and having free roam. When you do this, you are asking for accidents, destruction of your personal items, and a constant headache of wondering where your puppy is and what he is getting into next.

When a pup is given free roam, he will take full advantage of everything and anything. **This is why I stress that you must create structure and set boundaries on your pup for him to learn what is right and appropriate.** The sooner your dog learns these and adheres to these principles, the sooner he will be able to have freedom and free roam without you needing to worry about what he is getting into or if he's having an accident while you're not looking. And, in my opinion, properly crate training is the best way to achieve structure as a means to grant more freedom.

Once you feel comfortable and confident that your dog understands what is appropriate behavior, then you can begin to transition your dog out of the crate and gradually grant more and more freedom. As always, this process will certainly depend upon the dog. Some may start misbehaving after more freedom is granted, after which you'll need to return back to the crate and utilizing structure, while others may transition quicker.

With that being said, wherever your dog stands with his crate training, it's crucial that you *never* use the crate as punishment when he misbehaves. Doing this will completely disrupt the crate training process as it defeats the entire purpose of the exercise—to create a calming environment where your dog can feel safe and secure. Having a control area for your dog is the first step in teaching self-control and other desirable behaviors, which cannot be achieved if you associate this area with fear or negativity.

Below is a tentative schedule of how to revolve a puppy's day around the crate:

- Puppy wakes up in crate and goes straight outside to go potty ➔

- Puppy goes back in crate to eat breakfast and stays for 30-60 minutes to let food digest ➔

- Puppy goes straight outside again to go potty ➔

- Since your puppy has now gone potty, you can be sure that he won't have an accident inside. Puppy can now have an hour of playtime under your supervision (Keep in mind that when a puppy is out of the crate, he should be taken outside EVERY 20 minutes to go potty) →

- Puppy can now go in crate with chewing object for 1-2 hours →

- Puppy goes straight outside to go potty →

- Puppy goes back to crate for lunch for 20-30 minutes →

- Puppy goes outside to go potty →

- Puppy gets playtime under your supervision →

- Puppy goes in crate for nap/chew time →

- Puppy goes straight outside to go potty →

- Puppy goes back to crate for dinner for 20-30 minutes →

- Puppy goes outside to go potty →

- Puppy gets playtime under your supervision →

- Puppy goes outside to go potty right before bed →

- Puppy gets tucked into his crate for bedtime.

House Training Your Pup

························ 🐾 ························

House training is one of the hardest parts of raising a puppy for many new dog owners. However, if done correctly and consistently, it doesn't have to be so time-consuming and frustrating! Follow my advice, and it can be VERY simple. Simplicity aside, don't come into this step with unrealistic expectations or time lines such as "I want my puppy to be house trained in three days." This type of impractical thinking sets you up for disappointment and will only cause you to get discouraged if your puppy doesn't learn as quickly as you'd hoped.

As I've CONSTANTLY mentioned throughout this book, your dog is an individual that responds to training at his OWN pace, based on a myriad of reasons unique to YOUR pup. Therefore, don't be influenced by the marketing pitches of training programs that tell you they can "train any dog in six days or less." This training process requires patience, understanding, and trust. With that being said, let's get down to the nitty-gritty of how to house train your puppy the right way.

KEYS TO SUCCESS

Don't come into this step with unrealistic expectations or timelines such as "I want my puppy to be house trained in __ days." Understanding that your puppy is unique in how he will respond to training will put you at ease and in a better mindset to effectively and efficiently train your pup.

Q *When should I start house training my pup?*

You must be prepared to begin housetraining the second you bring the puppy home. Follow these guidelines to train your puppy in the fastest way possible and minimize the number of accidents your puppy has in your home.

Begin by showing your puppy the designated potty area you have chosen for him, which will be the place you bring him every time you go outside. He obviously will not go potty in that exact spot every time, but take him to that place right away when you bring him outside. He will eventually learn that when you bring him there, you want him to go potty! After doing that enough times, he will make the connection that outside is where you want him to go potty.

Q *How long can a puppy hold it before he needs to go potty?*

The amount of time that a dog can wait before having to go potty does vary depending on his age. Despite this fact, I always tell my clients that no matter how old a puppy is when you bring him home, be prepared to start housetraining from the very beginning as if he is an eight-week old puppy. Prevention is the best way to potty train, which in my opinion means taking your pup outside EVERY 20 MINUTES when he is out of his crate.

I have heard many people tell me things such as, "Well the people who cared for him previously said that he is doing great with potty training and only needs to go out every four hours." It's wonderful that he was doing so well with his former caregivers but by bringing him home into this brand new environment, everything is starting over for him, and you need to start over with him too. If he was doing well with housetraining previously, that is great and means that he should catch on quickly at your home also. **As a general rule of thumb, a puppy under one year old can typically hold it for how many months old he is + 1 HOUR.**

Q *So how often should I take my new puppy out to go potty?*

Again, when bringing a new puppy home, no matter what age, be prepared to bring him outside EVERY 20 MINUTES when out of the crate. Yes, every 20 minutes. **The more you can prevent accidents in the house, and the more times your puppy goes potty outside, the faster your pup will become housetrained.** When your puppy is consistently not having ANY accidents, you can then increase the time between potty breaks. If you are taking him out every 20 minutes consistently, you most likely will be able to increase the time between breaks after a week or two. Be sure to not jump the gun and increase the time too quickly; I suggest increasing by only 10-15 minute intervals at a time.

BRIGHT IDEAS

When house training a new puppy, set out to bring him outside to go to the bathroom every 20 minutes. Trust me, a shorter amount of time between potty breaks will teach your pup to become house trained faster because using shorter increments will decrease the chance of him having an accident. The less accidents your pup has and the more times he goes potty outside, the sooner he will start to make those neuron connections in his brain that going potty outside is a good thing.

Another tip I recommend is to **ALWAYS bring treats outside with you when you begin potty training.** I have my treat pouch hanging up at the door next to the dogs' leashes so that I always remember it when taking my foster puppies outside. I also have a bag of treats outside on the patio (as I do in every room) so that I can reward them immediately for going potty.

Q *What should I do when I bring my dog outside?*

This is a great question that is VERY important to understand. As with the rest of the training process, routines are extremely effective in reducing the time it takes to train your puppy. By establishing a consistent routine associated with a particular activity, it becomes ingrained as a habit in the puppy's cognitive processes. Were you born knowing to always brush your teeth after waking up? Absolutely not! You had to establish that habit by being taught to do it over a prolonged period of time. After hundreds of times practicing this routine, brushing your teeth became a habit. The same goes for dogs;

giving them a clear and straightforward routine helps them remember what to do and follow your commands more readily and consistently.

Here is a basic potty routine that will simplify this process for you and your pup:

🐾 Bring your puppy to his designated 'potty area.'

🐾 Tell him to "go potty."

🐾 Once he does, give him a treat to let him know that he did something good by going potty outside.

- Initially, be sure to give your puppy treats or physical affection every time he goes potty outside.

It's that simple! In addition, crate training and housetraining can go hand in hand to make both processes easier! One of my keys to effective potty training is that **every single time you take the puppy out of his crate, he should immediately go outside to go the bathroom.** If he's having accidents while walking from his crate to the door, I recommend carrying your puppy outside to avoid this issue.

KEYS TO SUCCESS

Use the simple process outlined above to establish a simple potty routine that teaches your puppy to go to the bathroom outside. Remember that in the beginning you should take your puppy outside to go the bathroom *immediately* after taking him out of his crate.

Q *Is it normal for my pup to have accidents in his crate?*

No! It's a dog's natural instinct to not go to the bathroom where he sleeps. However, in rare occasions, there are some dogs that don't possess this natural instinctual response. In cases like this, it makes it much harder to potty train because you don't have a control space. However, this simply reinforces how imperative it is to be letting your pup out frequently so that you can ingrain this habit and make it instinctual for him.

The bottom line is **you should never keep your puppy in a crate so long that he can't hold it and has an accident.** If this happens, it's very detrimental to the housetraining process. To be a responsible puppy parent, know how long your puppy can hold it, and never leave him in his crate longer than that. If you are not able to let him out to go potty, it is your job to make arrangements so that he can go outside and relieve himself.

If your puppy is still having accidents in his crate within an amount of time that you know he CAN hold it for, the crate may be too large. His crate should only be large enough that he can turn around in and lay down in it. Any larger, and he will designate one area of the crate as his "den" and another as a place to go potty.

As an example, I had a client who had their 12 week old Maltese puppy in a medium sized crate. This pup, however, was having 3-4 accidents in her crate per day. I suggested putting a partition in the crate to decrease the volume of the crate, which stopped the pup from having any future accidents.

BRIGHT IDEAS

Preparing your personal schedule with your puppy's housetraining schedule in mind will minimize the chance of your pup having an accident in his crate.

Q What if I take my puppy outside and he won't go potty?

First off, be patient. I always try to stay outside with a puppy for at least 15 minutes. The more time and patience you give him in the beginning, the faster he will go potty once outside and the faster he will be housetrained. If I have the time, I will stay out with a puppy for 30 minutes in the beginning stages of potty training if that is how long it is taking the pup to go potty. This time decreases the more times he goes outside and understands where he is supposed to go, so don't worry—you will not have to stand outside with your pup for that long every time!

If you take your puppy outside and wait for 15 minutes, but he still isn't going, put him back into his crate when you go back inside. Far too often do people bring their puppies outside, the puppy does not go to the bathroom, and then, 10 minutes later, has an accident in the house. To prevent this, just put him in the crate, wait 10 minutes, and then try taking him outside again. Repeat this process as necessary until he goes potty outside.

Something to keep in mind if you're encountering issues like this is that if your pup's designated potty area is in the same area that he plays, this may confuse him and cause him to think its playtime when its actually time to go potty. It's because of cases like this that I recommend commanding your pup to "go potty" so that he knows that's what you want him to do. If that's not enough, establish a completely unique area where your pup should go potty to remove any confusion from the problem.

NOTE: It's crucial that you physically go outside with your pup and see them go potty so that you know if they can have freedom when they go back inside—rather than just letting the pup out the back door and "hoping" that they went potty.

Q *So what should I do when accidents happen?*

This is one of the most common questions I receive from new dog owners. Good thing, too, because it is also one of the most important when you've never owned a puppy before. As the owner, how you respond to your puppy having an accident is incredibly important to successful housetraining.

If you catch your puppy going potty in the house:

1. RUN to your puppy.

2. Say "No" and pick him up.

3. Bring him outside to the designated potty area and tell him to "go potty."

Seriously, *run*! Whenever one of my puppies started squatting in the house, I sprinted to the pup to try to catch him before he started going! Even if he is already going, get to him as fast as you can and pick him up. He will stop going once you pick him up, so don't be hesitant. Get him outside to his spot as fast as you can!

These are the ONLY three steps to take when your puppy has an accident. This. Is. It. Do not allow yourself to scold your pup if he has an accident. **Your pup will NOT respond well to negative reinforcement and excessive scolding, and it WILL stall the house training process.**

KEYS TO SUCCESS

How you respond to your puppy having an accident is paramount to how successful you will be in house training him. Remember these steps:

- RUN to your puppy.
- Say "No" and pick him up.
- Bring him outside to the designated potty area and tell him to "go potty."

NEVER:

- Rub your puppy's nose in his accident.
- Put your puppy in the crate as punishment for having an accident.
- Yell or aggressively scold your puppy.
- Just watch your puppy have an accident and not do anything about it.
- Scold your puppy for an accident you didn't see him do.

Of these myths, the last one is probably the most common mistake. **Many people will find a pile of poop or a puddle of urine in the house, get upset, and then scold the puppy for doing it. When you do this, your puppy has NO idea why you are scolding him.** By this point, he doesn't even remember going to the bathroom in the house! Scolding him will NOT benefit either of you in any way. So, unfortunately, there is really nothing to do in this situation other than to clean it up.

Upon reading this list, you may think to yourself, "Well…my Dad used to rub my dog's nose in his accident," or, "I heard that yelling at your puppy when he has an accident teaches him that he's not supposed to go in the house." While these are typical responses I get as a dog trainer, they couldn't possibly be more misguided. Myths such as these truly hurt dog owner's relationships with their pups because they alienate and scare their pups—often when they don't even know what they did wrong!

Debunking myths such as these is one of my primary motivations for writing this book. If I can prevent a new dog owner from making the same costly mistakes that have hurt thousands of other dog owners in the past, then I will have truly made a difference in improving the quality of relationships between dog owners and their pups.

Teaching Your Dog To Focus, Hear, and Understand Your Voice

.... 🐾 ....

After setting a basic training foundation for your puppy's living space, we can finally move on to the fun parts of training: teaching your puppy commands and tricks! For your puppy to hear and respond to your commands, however, you MUST first explicitly teach him to recognize your commands so that he can learn to respond accordingly. There are two essential elements that you must establish with your puppy to create habitual responses to your commands: **focus and name recognition.**

KEYS TO SUCCESS

Make sure that you have taught your puppy how to focus as well as understand his name before establishing any commands or gestures associated with these commands.

The Power of Positive Reinforcement

I *firmly* believe that using positive reinforcement is the most effective and efficient method for training dogs. Positive reinforcement uses rewards, such as praise and/or treats, when your dog does something right.

Q *Why do you only recommend positive reinforcement?*

Let me ask you this: what would make *you* more determined and excited to complete a task?

1. If every time you completed a task, you were **praised** for doing it correctly.

2. If every time a task was assigned to you, you were automatically given a negative stimulus until you completed the task. Once you finish, the negative stimulus is removed, but there is no praise.

I think it's safe to say that most people would definitely find the first example more enjoyable of a task to complete!

The first example is an example of positive reinforcement, whereas the second is an example of negative reinforcement. In my experience, I have found that dogs respond significantly better to positive reinforcement than to negative reinforcement. Why? Knowing that a reward will be given to a dog once they complete a task correctly gives them motivation and excitement to complete the task, while providing positive energy. Like I said before, you want training to be FUN! Positive reinforcement keeps a dog in good spirits and creates a positive environment so that your pup will look forward to training.

Gaining Your Pup's Focus

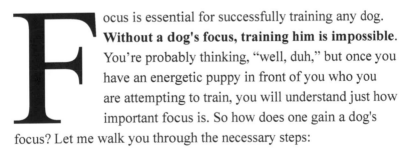

Focus is essential for successfully training any dog. **Without a dog's focus, training him is impossible.** You're probably thinking, "well, duh," but once you have an energetic puppy in front of you who you are attempting to train, you will understand just how important focus is. So how does one gain a dog's focus? Let me walk you through the necessary steps:

- Begin with just you and your pup in a room.

  - **If your puppy is still in the beginning stages of training, choose a room without any toys or noise;** somewhere with the least amount of distractions.

- Make sure you have your treats split up into small pieces.

- If your pup is more focused on his surroundings, show him a treat by putting it up to his nose, pull the treat back to you, and then give him the treat when he looks at you.

- Yes, that's right — **give him a treat for doing *nothing* but being focused on you.**

- You want your pup to think: "When I am focused on Mom or Dad, I get a treat."

If at *any* time during a training session it seems like your puppy is just so distracted or not listening to you, come back to focus.

- **Whenever your dog comes back to focusing on you for a few seconds or more, automatically give him a treat and use your clicker word.**

  ★ If your puppy looks at you <u>after you say his name or make a noise</u>, give him **one** treat.

  ★ If your pup looks at you <u>on his own at any time</u>, give him **two** treats.

  ★ This will help keep his attention on you knowing that he will be rewarded for just focusing on you.

KEYS TO SUCCESS

Gaining your dog's focus is absolutely <u>mandatory</u> for successful obedience training . Without a pup's focus, training is impossible.

Remember that these guidelines vary depending on where your puppy is at with his training. I am starting at the very beginning, as if your puppy has NEVER been introduced to these exercises. Therefore, you can adjust your protocol once your puppy becomes more trained in order to make him work harder for treats once his skills advance.

Focus has always been my most important tool for training. The first session I have with a new client, I constantly reward a dog for focusing on me. As I said before, focus is often overlooked. When a puppy is just sitting in front of his owner, looking up and focusing on his owner, this is the most important thing you could reward your pup for. If you always have your dog's focus, you can make him do anything AND prevent him from misbehaving.

🐾 Getting Your Pup To Understand Your Voice: Teaching Your Pup His Name

Once you decide on a name for your pup, stick with it so he can learn his name quickly. It took me almost a week to name Grizzly, which definitely made it harder to train him in the very beginning due to the fact that you can't begin to effectively train a pup until you teach him his name.

Bright Ideas

Be sure to decide on your puppy's name BEFORE beginning to train him

---

The first thing I tell dog owners when they get a new pup is to always associate the pup's name with positivity!

My second "Golden Rule" of dog training also happens to be the number one rule with teaching a pup his name, which is to associate his name with positivity. When using your pup's name, ALWAYS say it with a positive tone. This may sound like common sense, but it's *definitely* easier said than done. I can't tell you how many times I've caught Juneau doing something naughty and just want to yell "JUNEAU!" angrily at her. However, identifying your pup's name with negativity will only hurt the training process, *especially* if your dog is a little on the skittish side to begin with. Use "Leave It" or

"No!", and refrain from including your dog's name. Basically, you can use whatever scolding term you prefer as long as it is not the puppy's name.

It's very important to use words other than "No" for behaviors you don't want your dog performing. Why? Well, think about it like this: If all you ever say is "No," your puppy won't exactly understand what he is doing wrong. It's important to use a specific command for different unwanted actions that insinuate that he needs to stop, such as "Leave It" or "Off".

> *Bottom line, you want your puppy to know that his*
> *or her name means something good!*

If you want to get your puppy's attention, you will want your pup to happily look at you when you say his name instead of him running away from you in fear. When teaching your dog to 'Come' later in this section, you will definitely want to incorporate your puppy's name, and you will want the pup to happily come to you when his name is called. Imagine if every time your Mom or Dad called your name, you didn't know whether you would be in trouble or if it was for something good. Would you go happily to them every time? I definitely wouldn't!

KEYS TO SUCCESS

The number one rule with teaching your puppy his name is to ALWAYS associate his name with positivity.

Q *How do I teach my puppy his name?*

Teaching your puppy his name is going to be the easiest training exercise in this section, and it's a great place to start for both you and your pup to get associated with my training techniques. This exercise is also great practice for getting your pup to focus on you, which, as you now know, will be an extremely important tool to use for the rest of your puppy's life.

Keep in mind that the instructions below are for the first step of training your dog a new command that we discussed earlier:

🐾 Say your puppy's name.

🐾 As soon as he looks at you or comes to you, say the clicker word and reward him.

- Incorporate this into your daily routine constantly.

🐾 **For this exercise, your puppy's name is being used as the command to look at you.**

- For this reason, only say your puppy's name ONE time.

🐾 If he doesn't look right away, use the 'kissy noise' to get his attention.

- If it is taking him a long time to look at you, just wait patiently. He will eventually look up at you.

🐾 You may also experience the opposite — your puppy will not take his gaze off of you. **This is a good problem to have!**

- If this is the case, try hiding the treats so that your puppy can't see them and focus your gaze on something other than your puppy.

- If he sees you looking at something else, he might want to look too.

    ★ If he is still not looking away, **introduce some distractions**.

    ★ Set a toy on the other side of the room or have another person come into the room. Once he looks away, say his name.

    ★ Again, once he looks at you: clicker word and treat.

> Once your puppy gets the hang of this at home, try doing this in new locations. This exercise is *great* for introducing your puppy to new surroundings while teaching him to still keep his focus on you despite distractions.

❧ TEACHING YOUR DOG TO RESPOND AND LISTEN TO YOUR VOICE USING COMMANDS

Now that your puppy knows his name and you have gone through the first step of commanding him to look at you when called, you can begin moving through the rest of these basic commands.

BRIGHT IDEAS

Following the positive reinforcement guidelines throughout this handbook will give you infinitely greater results than when using negative reinforcement. Puppies are like humans in that they respond better when being praised for what they're doing right than scolded for their mistakes.

Get ready for the journey that lies ahead! Keep in mind the pep talk we had earlier about the reality of training your unique dog and **stay determined!** Also, always remember that you have this section — along with the rest of the book — to refer to as your puppy parenthood reference if you encounter any roadblocks along the way!

KEYS TO SUCCESS

As you continue to train your pup, remember that it's very normal to encounter difficulties along the way! Your puppy isn't going to listen to everything you say in the beginning perfectly. If you get frustrated, refer back to the teachings throughout this section to help you troubleshoot any problems you may come across.

Basic Obedience Training Commands:

- *Sit*
- *Lay Down*
- *Wait*

- *Come*
- *Stay*
- *Touch*

- *Shake*
- *Heel*
- *Leave It*

❧ Basic Commands — "Sit"

Teaching your puppy to sit is the next stepping-stone in getting him to become a well-trained dog. When a puppy can sit on command, it helps him with self-control. This method of teaching your puppy to sit will teach him not only to sit physically but also to calm down mentally and engage his focus on you. **Keep in mind that your dog needs to MASTER how to sit on command before moving on to the next exercises.** Many of the other commands begin with your dog sitting.

Learning to sit is **especially** helpful for high-energy pups who need a little help with self-control. You can sit or stand for this exercise, but if your puppy likes to jump all over you, you may want to stand.

THE "SIT" GESTURE

················· *How To Teach Your Pup To Sit:* ·················

1. Have your puppy facing you. Tell your puppy to "sit" while holding the treat in the hand position shown in the drawing above.

2. **After saying sit once, you *will NOT* repeat that word again.**

3. Put a treat to the puppy's nose.

4. Move your hand slowly forward (from your direction) towards the dog as if you are moving the treat over the puppy's head.

- This motion will make the puppy lower his butt and sit to obtain the treat.

5. Once his butt touches the floor, reward him with the clicker word and a treat.

6. Be sure that you are staying at your pup's pace and keeping the treat on his nose. I often see people luring faster than the dog is following

   - **NEVER force your puppy to sit by pushing his butt to the floor.**

     ★ This obviously doesn't teach your pup to sit on his own, and it can also damage his hips.

7. Repeat this exercise MANY times a day until learned.

Don't get discouraged if your puppy isn't sitting right away! It does take some puppies a little while to realize that he needs to lower his butt to the floor to get the treat when it's over his head. Be patient and persistent. If he starts giving up on the treat and is no longer focused on it, say his name or use the 'kissy noise' and start back in the position, you began in, with the treat touching his nose.

> NOTE: I have the commands in this order for a reason! As much as you may want to skip ahead to 'shake' because you think it's fun, if you are a new dog owner, PLEASE follow the commands in order. I have structured them so that you're gradually building up the difficulty level and not overwhelming your puppy with commands that are way too complicated for his current capabilities.

🐾 "Lay Down"

After your puppy has learned how to sit, he is ready to learn to lay down. **Don't start trying to teach your dog how to lay down until he knows how to "sit."** The reason for this is that your puppy will get confused if you try to teach him too many commands at once, and you need your dog to start in a sitting position to teach this command.

Begin by getting your puppy to sit in front of you. Next, hold a treat in one hand and, with the other hand, signal him to "lay down" with the hand gesture shown below:

THE "LAY DOWN" GESTURE

·············· *How To Teach Your Pup To Lay Down:* ··············

1. Put the treat up to his nose and slowly start luring your pup down by moving your hand down to the floor aiming for between his paws.

    *   Remember that luring should always be at your dog's pace.

2. Once your hand hits the floor, slowly move it towards you and away from him along the floor.

    *   This motion should lower him into the laying down position.

3. Once he lays down, say your clicker word and give him a treat.

4. Repeat this exercise MANY times until learned.

This command forces dogs to focus for a longer amount of time before receiving the treat. While this sometimes causes puppies to give up before you even get your hand to the final position, this is OK!

Q *What should I do if my puppy gives up before I finish?*

IF this happens:

1. Move your hand back to where your puppy left off.

2. If he isn't meeting you back in this position, **start over at the beginning with the treat touching his nose.**

    *   NOTE: It took Grizzly four training sessions of this exercise before he actually did it!

3. Continue until your puppy lays down.

4. Resume with the prior protocol: after he lies down, say the clicker word and give him a treat.

5. Repeat MANY times until learned.

Don't get discouraged if it seems like your puppy is not responding to your commands! I swear it finally clicks with them unexpectedly just when you think they will never learn it. Be patient! **Even if it doesn't seem like the puppy is making progress, he most certainly is. Every training session is part of the process and is helping him learn the command.**

Just as it often takes a person multiple sessions to learn something new the first time they try—whether a new sport, hobby or skill—dogs learn in the SAME way. Therefore, don't hold your puppy to a higher standard than you would yourself! Be understanding of your pup's learning curve, and it will make the ENTIRE training process a whole lot more enjoyable for BOTH of you!

❧ "STAY"

Teaching your puppy to stay is a PRICELESS training tool to possess in your training arsenal. It's also one of the commands that usually takes puppies a little longer to learn because it requires a LOT of self-control and a much longer attention span than the previous commands.

I find that it is easiest to have your pup stay in the lay down position. They are not as apt to want to move when they are laying down than they are when sitting, but you can teach your pup to stay in either position! Next, command your puppy to 'stay' and give him the stay hand signal:

THE "STAY" GESTURE

You will keep this hand signal out the entire exercise while your puppy is just learning this command.

.... *How To Teach Your Pup To Stay:* ....

1. With your hand out, take a step back with both feet.

2. Return back to your starting position in front of your pup.

3. If your puppy stays seated the entire time, reward him with the clicker word and a treat.

   - High-energy puppies are a lot more likely to not want to stay seated. If your puppy gets up before you return back in front of him, tell him "uh-uh" and get him back into a seated position.

   - You may not get further than one step for the first few training sessions and this is alright!

4. Next, try taking two steps back.

5. Keep increasing the distance that you walk away from your pup as long **as he continues to stay seated and doesn't move.**

   - If your puppy moves out of the seated position, say "uh-uh" and get him back into the seated position.

   - At your next attempt, command him to 'stay' and then decrease the number of steps you take.

6. Continue to move back as far as you'd like until you feel your puppy understands the commands.

7. Repeat this exercise MANY times until learned.

❀ "WAIT"

Wait is an underused but incredibly useful command to have at your disposal as a dog owner. It can be applied to teaching your puppy to wait for his food, wait for you to take off his leash, open his crate, etc. **In every possible way you use this command, "wait" teaches your pup patience and self-control.** Teaching your pup self-control is key to having a well-trained dog in almost every area of obedience. Definitely take the time to teach your pup this command.

Put your puppy in whatever position you would like him to wait in. **Either sitting or lying down is the most ideal.**

THE "WAIT" COMMAND

.... *How To Teach Your Pup To Wait* ···············
(Using The Example Of Giving A Treat Or Food):

1. Tell him to "wait" and use the wait hand signal.

2. While your pup is in the seated position—preferably in his crate (because feedings should take place there)—slowly lower the food bowl down to him.

3. If he starts to jump or attempts to get at the bowl in any way, say "uh-uh" and raise the bowl back up.

4. Get him back into the seated position and start again.

    - **With high-energy puppies, you will most likely have to do this many, many times in just one exercise.**

    - Do not set down his food bowl until he has patiently waited for you to lower it without getting out of the seated position.

        * It may take a long time, so be patient!

5. After you set the food bowl down, try to keep him waiting for another second, and then say "OK."

    - If he starts going for the food before you tell him "OK," tell him "uh-uh," pick up the bowl, and try again.

        ★ **"OK" is the release word and communicates to your puppy that it is okay for him to stop waiting and eat the food that you've placed in front of him.**

    - As you keep practicing "Wait," lengthen the amount of time between setting the bowl down and saying, "OK."

6. Repeat this exercise MANY times until learned.

❧ "Come"

Training your puppy to come to you when called is the single most valuable and important command you can teach him. This command is also one that many puppy owners neglect to teach, which leads to issues down the road as the dog ages and cements poor habits.

Q *Why is teaching my dog to come to me so important?*

"Come" is a command that will be foundational for the rest of your pup's life. Think of how many times you may need your pup to come to you when you call and all the different situations, frustrations, or even danger that could arise if he doesn't come. Therefore, don't make the mistake of skipping over this crucial command. While it may take longer than other commands for your puppy to learn to come, it is absolutely worth the time investment.

·········· *How To Teach Your Pup To Come:* ··········

1. When teaching this command, start in an enclosed area so that your pup does not have freedom to run if he chooses not to obey.

2. Take your pup off of his leash and allow him to roam around.

3. Say your puppy's name followed by the command "Come" in a very positive voice while holding out a treat.

    • Always associate the command with positivity!

        ★ **You want your dog to always come when he's called, and for that to happen, your pup needs to think that**

something positive will *always* happen when he comes to you.

4. If your pup doesn't come to you right away, make a 'kissy noise' or other attention grabbing noise to make sure he sees the treat. Be patient and redirect his attention to you until he comes.

5. **When he *does* come to you, reward him with the clicker word and a treat, no matter how long it takes him to do it.**

6. Repeat this exercise MANY times until learned.

"FLUFFY, COME!"

Fluffy looks at his owner but decides that running off in the opposite direction sounds like more fun.

Does this scenario sound familiar to you?

Then you are in the same boat as many, many other dog owners.

One of the hardest aspects of training for owners seems to be teaching their dog recall.

From their home, to the dog park and everywhere in between—owners have a difficult time getting their dog to consistently come to them!

In a perfect scenario, the owner commands the dog: "come!", and the dog drops whatever he is doing at any given moment to come to his owner.

Q *What if I told you that you can have this perfect scenario ALL the time?*

Yes, your dog does have the ability to come to you when called, I promise you! It just takes a few simple steps.

1. The first step of recall training is to associate "come" with nothing but positivity.

- What does your dog associate the word "come" with?

- Does "come" mean that it is time to leave the dog park?

- Or does it mean that it is bath time?

- Or does it mean that it is time to go in his crate for the night?

- If your dog associates "come" with these types of actions, why would he want to come to you?

This is the key to successful recall training: Making your dog want and choose to come to you!

How do you do this?

By making the command mean **nothing but positivity and rewards.**

2. The second your dog comes to you after you call him, you need to REWARD him.

- Remember that rewards can be attention, affection, toys, treats, etc...

- But for this command, specifically, you want to use a highly motivating reward — sometimes I even recommend using "special" treats that you only use during recall training.

The reason that you have to use highly motivating treats at first is because to get your dog to want to do something, you need to motivate him.

When your dog is off leash exploring outside, his freedom and free roam is very motivating in itself.

Therefore, to be able to get your dog's attention and to make him want to come to you, you may need to motivate him using an object of his desire when first beginning recall training.

However, if the only time you ever tell your dog to "come" is when you are going to end the play time by putting on his leash and restricting his freedom, teaching this command is going to be an uphill battle for you.

Instead, telling your dog to "come" throughout your stay at the dog park or another fun place, and consistently *rewarding* him for coming will teach your dog to associate coming to you when called with a reward; as opposed to the negative consequence of leaving such a fun place!

Another common objection I get is "Well, if I only motivate my dog with treats, then they're not going to listen to me; they only want the treats, and won't listen to me when I don't have food to give them."

This is why transitioning out of treats becomes key, and showing your dog that listening to you and pleasing YOU as their pack leader is the biggest reward there is.

After gaining your dog's motivation and attention with praise and treats, slowly begin to wean off the treats in your training until you get to the point where your fur friend will come when called on a whim—not because you're holding a treat in your hand... but because he respects you!

Another very important part of recall training that is often overlooked is starting small and working your way up.

When a client tells me that their dog will not come when at the dog park, I ask how their recall is at home?

Some respond that the dog always comes, and some say that he comes when he wants.

This is a crucial situation to analyze in your own life.

If your dog does not come every single time you command him to "come" at home, how can you expect your dog to come to you while at the dog park?! You can't!

Home is where the dog is most familiar with his surroundings, and there are the fewest distractions.

The dog park is on the other end of the spectrum, where there are a million and one distractions, and your dog probably has a harder time keeping self control.

If your dog does not have a good basis of recall at home, he will not consistently respond to your recall anywhere else.

Therefore, start the training by practicing recall where there are the fewest distractions and slowly increase the distractions to make it more challenging.

And if your pup doesn't come right away and instead runs off, never scold him for coming back to you! He will eventually end up coming to you, and if you scold him, he will associate the scolding and negativity with him coming back to you. This is obviously the opposite of what you want so do *everything* in your power to refrain from scolding during recall training. I know how frustrating it can be when your dog is not obeying you and running off but when he does come back to you, make sure it's not a negative experience for him.

🐾 "Leave It"

Leave it is certainly a beneficial command to use with puppies, considering they typically want to get into everything and be adventurous!

🦴 You will use this command when your pup is going toward something you don't want him getting into.

This key command will come in handy many, many times throughout your pup's life.

················ *How To Teach Your Pup To "Leave It":* ················

METHOD 1

1. Whenever your pup starts going for or is already getting into something you don't want him to get at, firmly tell him "Leave It"

2. Remember to only say the command once! Use the "kissy" sound, his name, or any other sound to get his attention

3. If your pup doesn't respond, put a treat or toy on his nose and lure him over to you

4. Once he does leave the object, tell him "Yes" or the clicker word of your choice and reward him

5. Remember that it is very important to have an extra motivating reward, so that he is motivated every time to leave the object no matter what it is or how enticing it may be!

> **METHOD 2**

1. Have your pup start laying down

2. Put a treat on the ground (covered by your hand, or uncovered, depending on the difficulty level he is at)

3. Tell your pup to "Leave it"

4. Once he looks at you, tell him "Yes" and reward him with a treat from the other hand

5. Remember it is important to practice this so that he thinks: "If I leave this, I get something better"

THE "LEAVE IT" COMMAND

KEYS TO SUCCESS

It's important to sometimes use words other than "NO" for behaviors you don't want your puppy performing. This way, your puppy can distinguish what exactly it is that he's doing wrong.

❧ "Touch"

Touch is my *favorite* command! Touch teaches your pup to target something and touch it with his nose. It is a really good exercise to get your pup's brain moving and another great way to keep his focus where you want it. Also, **touch is the first step in teaching your dog to target specific things** such as ringing a bell when he has to go outside. Plus, I think it's so cute when they touch their cute noses to my hand.

THE "TOUCH" GESTURE

·········· *How To Teach Your Pup To Touch:* ··········

1. As always, begin with your dog sitting while facing you.

2. Hold a treat in one hand.

3. Command your dog to "Touch" and hold your other hand (without the treat) out flat in front of your dog's nose, while also holding a treat in the other hand. Once your dog starts to get the hang of this command, you will not need to have a treat in your hand, and your hand signal for touch will look like the drawing.

4. In the beginning, hold your hand about six inches away from your dog's nose.

5. As soon as your dog's nose touches your hand, reward him with the clicker word and a treat from your OTHER hand.

6. You will never give your dog the treat in the hand he touched.

7. If your dog is getting the hang of it right away, remove the treat altogether.

8. Keep moving your hand higher above your dog's nose to make the exercise more difficult.

9. Repeat this exercise MANY times until mastered.

THE "TOUCH" GESTURE

❧ "SHAKE"

Who wouldn't want their dog to be able to give them a pawshake??
Shake is a fun command to teach, but I have found that it takes most
puppies a while to learn. As always, be patient and persistent. Work on
this <u>every day</u> with your pup.

THE "SHAKE" GESTURE

·········· *How To Teach Your Pup To Shake:* ··········

1. Begin with your dog sitting while facing you.

2. Command your pup to "shake" and make the shake hand gesture
   like the drawing above.

3. Place the treat right up to one side of your pup's chest.

- This one takes patience and can be harder for the puppy to learn what exactly you are trying to get him to do.

- Most pups will bite at the treat and do whatever they can to try to get it.

4. **As soon as your puppy paws at the treat or just lifts his paw, *immediately* reward him with the clicker word and treat.**

5. Repeat this exercise MANY times until learned.

For this exercise, if your pup ends up standing up and getting out of the seated position, it's okay. Once he associates the reward with lifting his paw up, he will realize that it is easiest to lift his paw while seated. However, each time you begin the exercise again, get him into a seated position first.

❀ "Heel"

Teaching your dog to heel can be one of the most beneficial skills your dog will ever learn. If you start working on this command with your dog when he's still young, you can beat the odds and have a dog that actually knows how to heel while walking on a leash!

One of the most common behavioral problems that I run into with my clients is pulling while walking on the leash. **Teaching your pup to heel can avoid these future issues and provide for a much enjoyable walk for both you and your pup.**

············ Some Tips For Loose Leash Walking: ············

🐕 **As always, use positive reinforcement.**

- I'm reiterating this for heel in particular because it's very easy to get frustrated and stray away from positive reinforcement while teaching this command!

🐕 **Always walk with a loose leash.**

- You never want to be walking with a tightened leash between you and your dog.

  ★ You want there to be slack in the leash so there's no pull or strain on either end of the leash.

🐕 **Be consistent with what side your dog walks on.**

- This is something that many dog owners overlook and they end up with a pup who zigs and zags all over the place (walking back and forth on each side of you).

- Choose a side (right or left) of you that feels most comfortable to have your dog walk on and stick with it.

············ How To Teach Your Pup To Heel: ············

1 **Position the leash as in the example above.**

2 **If your pup is on your right side, hold the end of the leash with your left hand and then grab it with your right hand down by your side.**

   - If your pup is on your left side, flip those instructions.

3 **If your puppy stays right by your side, a second hand holding the leash isn't necessary. You only have to hold the leash at the end with one hand.**

4   **Get into a position where your pup is on your side and you have his attention.**

5   **Try to get him as calm and focused as possible before beginning to teach him the command.**

   • Have him sit by your side and reward him with the clicker word and a treat.

6   **Say your puppy's name and then tell him "HEEL."**

7   **Keep looking at your puppy as you continue to walk.**

8   **Any time he looks up at you, automatically say the clicker word.**

   • Depending on how often he's looking up at you, you can give him a treat with the clicker word every time or every other time. The more frequently your dog demonstrates focus by looking up at you, the less and less you'll use treats as a reward, as opposed to stopping treats altogether at once. This is done in order to wean off of treat training in the right way, that is, gradually replacing treats with solely your clicker word and praise.

9   **Take one step forward and try to keep your pup's attention.**

10 **Ideally, he will stay next to you and heel instead of trying to pull forward.**

   • If he's losing his focus on you at any time, say his name or make the kissy noise, but do not repeat the command more than once.

   • If your puppy's focus is staying on you and the leash is still loose, keep walking.

11 **If your puppy pulls forward and tightens the leash, STOP walking!**

1 2 You want your puppy to walk back to you and loosen the leash.

- If he doesn't do this right away, say his name or the kissy noise.

- If he doesn't come back to you, take a step back.

  ★ He should follow.

- If he still isn't coming back to you, lure him back with a treat.

1 3 Once he is finally back next to you, tell him the clicker word and give him a treat.

1 4 Repeat this exercise MANY times until learned.

> You want to make sure you are using a treat that your pup goes crazy for, especially for this command because you NEED to keep his attention and focus despite everything going on around him.

If your pup is VERY resistant to walking on the leash, I strongly suggest using a harness when teaching him how to heel and just for introducing him to leash walking in general. This is something I had to do with Grizzly when he was a pup. In the beginning, he would stop in his tracks and sit and didn't want to move one centimeter while attached to a leash. At this time, he was also still fearful of all humans (including me), so I couldn't even lure him to me with a treat. However, once he got comfortable with leash walking, he began to LOVE his walking and hiking time.

BRIGHT IDEAS

Notice that I didn't include any "Keys To Success" or "Bright Ideas" throughout these commands? That's because every single step is SO important. When you need help on any of these commands, go back to the steps I've provided you. All of the answers you need are there!

Solving The 20 TOUGHEST Dog Behavioral Problems

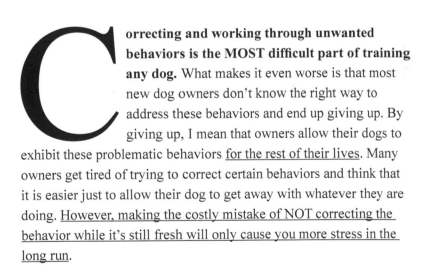

Correcting and working through unwanted behaviors is the MOST difficult part of training any dog. What makes it even worse is that most new dog owners don't know the right way to address these behaviors and end up giving up. By giving up, I mean that owners allow their dogs to exhibit these problematic behaviors <u>for the rest of their lives</u>. Many owners get tired of trying to correct certain behaviors and think that it is easier just to allow their dog to get away with whatever they are doing. <u>However, making the costly mistake of NOT correcting the behavior while it's still fresh will only cause you more stress in the long run.</u>

Q *But it just seems so difficult… how can I do it?*

YOU MUST BE PATIENT. I am going to address the most common dog behavioral issues and give you the most effective and efficient methods in the obedience-training field to solve them. Just remember, like every aspect of dog training, each dog is unique and will respond to training methods differently. Some will catch on right away, while others may take weeks to fully understand that a behavior is not appropriate. You MUST be patient. Whether you only have to tell your pup twice not to do something or you have to say it 50 times, PATIENCE IS KEY. This rule is easy to remember right now, but the tricky part is remembering while you are trying to correct your puppy for doing something inappropriate. Refer to this section when you need to refocus.

YOU MUST BE STRICT. Sometimes owners feel bad for having to tell their dog "No". Don't! If a dog is misbehaving, then he needs to be told that what he is doing is wrong and redirected to what is appropriate. IT IS TOTALLY OKAY TO TELL YOUR DOG "NO." There's no need for excessive or aggressive scolding, but do not be afraid to tell your pup "NO" firmly. Remember that every "NO" is to be followed with redirection. Be strict from the start with what's acceptable and what's not, or your dog will walk all over you.

YOU MUST BE CONSISTENT. I can't stress this one enough. It goes hand in hand with the last point because you must be strict about what is acceptable and what isn't EVERY SINGLE TIME. If you don't, all the time you put into establishing strict obedience will be wasted. If you are attempting to teach your puppy that something isn't appropriate, you must correct him EVERY time he exhibits that behavior.

I see many dog owners allowing their puppies to perform certain inappropriate behaviors at times and then scold the puppy for it other times. For example, owners often allow their pups to jump up on them with open arms when they arrive home from work, but then scold their pup just hours later when Fido jumps on a guest. This inconsistency only confuses the pup by clouding the difference between what you consider right and wrong—which will lengthen or even stall the training process altogether. Decide what you deem as inappropriate right away, stick to it, and be consistent.

Q *Do I have to fix it now?*

You don't, but do take into consideration that **it's substantially easier to correct a puppy's inappropriate behavior than an adult dog's.** Again, it's much, much easier to redirect a puppy to the appropriate behavior than it is to correct an adult dog's misbehavior. An adult dog who's been performing inappropriate behaviors has been doing it his whole life and has reinforced this habit thousands of times, making it incredibly difficult to break. On the other hand, a puppy's brain is still developing and learning what is right and what's not. It's worth it to invest the time into training your puppy the right way, as opposed to taking more time and effort to correct your dog's behavior later on.

KEYS TO SUCCESS

You must be patient, strict and consistent as you work on correcting your puppy's behavioral problems. Put in the hard work and discipline that this step requires and you WILL be rewarded with a well-behaved dog.

Think about it like this, would you rather spend a few hours TODAY fixing your puppy's digging, barking, or other problem? Or, would you rather wait a few YEARS of painstaking frustration to finally hire a dog trainer for thousands of dollars to fix your dog's problem, when it could've been nipped in the bud before it even got to that point? When you look at the situation like this, it becomes an obvious and simple decision—sacrifice a bit of comfort and ease NOW for a LIFETIME of gratification with your dog.

> **BRIGHT IDEAS**
>
> Make a goal for correcting your puppy's problem <u>and stick with it</u>. As you work toward your goal, use the following guide to diagnose and solve the specific behavioral problem you want to stop.

I do understand that this sacrifice I'm describing is much easier to write about than actually DO. I know that we live in an instant-gratification world, where people are incredibly impatient and undervalue the purpose of long-term investment in something worthwhile.

Nonetheless, I am asking you to make a decision that you won't regret—going through the trouble of fixing your puppy's behavioral problem(s) now, and not giving up! Whether you are already at the point of desperation with your puppy's problems, or you just made the wise decision to take responsibility for your puppy's actions, buckle up and prepare for the adversities that may lie ahead. I commend you for taking the first step towards raising the dog of your dreams. While this journey will be arduous, feel at ease that you have my knowledge and experience to guide you through it. If you ever need me, I'm just an email away. ♥

The 20 TOUGHEST Dog Behavioral Problems

- Mouthiness
- Jumping Up On People
- Destructive Chewing
- Pulling While On Leash
- Not Wanting To Walk On A Leash
- Uncontrollable Rough-housing and Zooming
- Separation Anxiety
- Fearfulness
- Bolting And Escaping
- Coprophagy (Eating Poop)

- Excessive Barking & Whining
- Jumping On Furniture
- Digging
- Begging
- Playing Too Rough
- Herding Other Dogs Or People
- Reactivity
- Aggression
- Resource Guarding From People
- Resource Guarding From Other Dogs

🐾 Mouthiness:

You might think a puppy being mouthy with your hand is cute when he is eight weeks old, but how do you think you'll feel when you have a larger and stronger adult dog biting at your hand?

Mouthing (which includes nipping and biting) is a behavior that a majority of puppies exhibit. It comes from a dog's need to chew and not entirely knowing how to control their bite inhibition.

The thing is, puppies are not born to know the difference between a chew toy and your hand. Therefore, you have to teach them what is appropriate to chew on and what is not. So although you may think it's cute when your tiny puppy is mouthing on your hand, **don't EVER let your pup chew or mouth on you!** From the second you bring your puppy home, make sure he knows that you and your clothes are not to be chewed.

If your puppy is trying to mouth or chew on you or your clothing:

1. Tell your puppy "No."

2. Redirect him to an appropriate chewing item (chew toy or bone)

As you can see, there are only two steps—correcting this behavior is quite simple in most cases. **However, the problem that I see with most puppy owners is a lack of consistency and persistence!** If you let your pup mouth on your hand one day and the next day you reprimand him for it, he will be confused and won't understand why you are telling him not to do something that you allowed him to do previously. Consistently tell him "no" from the start and you will see results.

In some extreme cases, however, you may find that redirection is not enough and your pup is still trying to mouth after redirecting him to a chewing item.

In this case:

🐾 Redirect him to 'sit' and focus on you before resuming play.

🐾 If your pup is still trying to mouth or nip you after doing this, put him in the crate to take a mental break and calm down.

🐾 Repeat these steps until the mouthing subsides.

- This is why I stressed the importance of proper crate training earlier in the book. When you create a control area for your pup (the crate) using positive reinforcement, it can be utilized as a training tool and as a positive area where your pup can relax and calm down when naughty behaviors arise.

Also, make sure that you are being firm when telling your pup that this behavior is not acceptable. I often witness the following two scenarios with my clients:

1. The puppy is sitting in the owner's lap and being mouthy. The owner says nothing. This is like nails on a chalkboard to me! I see many puppy owners get somewhat immune to the gentle puppy biting and then complain once the pup grows and the mouthing/biting begins to hurt. Do not let this be you! Act quickly to correct this behavior so that your pup quickly learns that this is not appropriate.

2. In the same scenario as #1, instead of saying nothing, the owner tells the puppy "No", but doesn't follow through with the correction. By this, I mean that the owner is sitting on the floor with the pup, tells him "No" when he mouths, the pup stops for a couple seconds, and then goes right back to mouthing. In this

case, "No" means nothing to the pup because the owner still made himself available to be a chew toy. Your pup needs to know that if he is going to continue to play inappropriately, he does not get the honor to play with you. This is like the parent who tells their child that he is grounded, yet continues to let him go out with his friends and do as he pleases. There are no boundaries in this scenario! If you want to see noticeable change in your pup, you really have to enforce the meaning behind "No".

Q *What if my puppy is gentle when he mouths?*

No matter what you have read other places, DO NOT encourage your puppy to play with you using his mouth. A lot of people ask me: "Well isn't it alright if he is playing with my hands gently?" **No, it is not alright!** There are a few reasons for this:

🐾 Your hands aren't meant to be a toy for dogs.

- **No matter how "gentle" your dog may be, your hands should NEVER be inside his mouth. Puppies have razor sharp teeth!**

🐾 You don't want your dog being mouthy with other people.

- Most people aren't familiar enough with dogs to know the difference between mouthing and biting.

  ★ If you have a puppy that mouths on other people, it could really scare them and be embarrassing for you!

🐾 Puppies often get overly excited to the point where they lack or completely lose self-control.

- When this happens, your pup may get SO excited that he forgets that the thing in his mouth is only to be played with "gently."

- **He may get so caught up in his excitement that he confuses your hand with a chew toy and bites down.**

- And let me tell you, those sharp puppy teeth HURT! So, by not allowing your hands to ever be in your puppy's mouth, you avoid all of this completely.

🐾 JUMPING UP ON PEOPLE:

Does your dog love to jump up on you and/or other people?

For those of you who are thinking: "Yes Fluffy just loves me so much and is so excited when I get home that she jumps up on me to give me a hug"...

...Did you know that jumping up on people is actually a behavioral issue that you should not encourage?

In fact, this behavior is one of the most common behavioral issues I see with my clients who want to have a well-behaved dog.

Owners often have a lot of trouble with getting dogs (of all ages) to stop jumping up on them and other people. Often, I get asked...

Q *Is there anything really wrong with this?*

Like I referenced earlier, some dog owners tell me that they don't mind that their puppy jumps up on them. If this is you, you need to think about this:

It may not seem like that big of a deal now and you may even think it is cute, but will you mind when your 80 pound dog is jumping on you? Chances are good that you will care when your dog knocks you down to the ground!

Or, if your puppy will only grow to be a smaller adult dog, do you want your dog jumping up on every person who walks through your door or every person who greets your dog?

Also, chances are good that you will have your dog out in public at some point... and there ARE people in this world that don't like dogs (they are absolutely insane, I know), and definitely don't want a dog jumping up on them.

Q Why does my dog like to jump on people?

The majority of the time, a dog will jump up on you or others out of excitement. Your pup gets excited when you walk through the door, and because he has not been taught to have self control when he is excited, he just throws his body up at you.

Another reason why a dog might jump up on you is if you are holding something that the dog wants. The dog thinks that he must jump up to let you know that he wants the item in your hand because he doesn't know any other way to tell you.

Q So what's the solution?

The most important thing that you can do when trying to correct this behavior is to NEVER allow your dog to jump up on anyone, EVER.

Often times I see people allow their dog to jump up on them sometimes, and then other times scold them for it.

Maybe one day you get home from work and are so excited to see your dog that you don't mind him jumping up and "hugging you," but the next day you are not in the mood for his jumping and scold him for it.

This does absolutely nothing but confuse your pup.

You MUST be consistent with what you deem as an appropriate behavior, and what is not appropriate, and strictly enforce it with your dog.

NOTE: If you do wish to teach your dog to "hug" on command, you have to nip the jumping up behavior FIRST and then can teach him that he is only allowed up on command.

The other common issue is owners telling me that they don't care if their pup jumps up on them, but they don't want their dog jumping on other people.

This is too confusing for dogs to understand!

They don't comprehend that they are able to jump on one person, but not others. What dogs *do* comprehend is that they are allowed to do something or that they are not allowed to do something altogether.

Not only is consistency crucial for teaching your pup to avoid this behavior, but it's also SO much easier to correct this behavior in puppies than in adult dogs for two reasons:

1. **It's a lot easier to curb this behavior when your pup is smaller and not as strong.**

2. **If an adult dog is having an issue with jumping on people, this likely means he's been allowed to jump up on people before.**

As I mentioned earlier, it's a lot harder to correct a behavior that a dog has been allowed to do his whole life than to train a puppy on what not to do. If you teach your puppy that jumping on people is not acceptable, you will not have to teach him this again as long as you continue to enforce it.

Q *So, how do I fix the jumping?*

As with every unwanted behavior, be strict from the start about not letting your pup jump up on you. **Again, NEVER let your pup jump up on you!** You probably have already figured out that this happens quite often when you are holding treats or something else that your pup wants. In this case, it is extremely important that you do not give your puppy the wanted object when he is jumping up on you.

If your puppy attempts to jump up on you:

🐾 Tell him "OFF."

🐾 Turn your body so that your back is facing your puppy.

🐾 When you move your body this way, your pup will automatically put his paws back down to the floor (where they belong).

🐾 Turn to face your pup again and redirect him to sit.

🐾 Once he sits, pet him and show him THIS is how he gets your attention.

🐾 If he starts jumping up on you again, stop giving him attention and repeat the steps above. Only give your puppy attention and affection when he is sitting.

🐾 Practice this routine until it becomes a habit for your pup to not jump up.

Eventually, your dog will learn that he will not get attention until he sits. This will keep him from jumping up, and it will also teach him to have self-control when he is excited.

Q *What should I do when I have guests over while I'm trying to train my pup?*

When you have guests in your home, inform your guests right away that you don't allow your pup to jump up on people and instruct them to turn their body and tell him "OFF" if he does.

Even further, I suggest taking control of the situation to prevent the jumping altogether. You can do this by putting your pup on a leash if you know that he is going to want to jump up on your guests. The reason that I first suggest using a leash is because without that added control, it's going to be extremely difficult for your dog to control himself to not jump up on someone, as the jumping is currently a self-rewarding behavior.

He thinks "no matter how I act, I'm going to be able to say 'Hi' to that person, so why should I try to control myself?" This is precisely why we want to completely prevent him from having the opportunity to jump up in the first place. If you start with the control of having your pup on a leash while going through the training, once you take him off leash it's going to be ingrained in him to sit before greeting someone.

It's also really great in general for your dog to get in the habit of controlling his excitement before greeting ANYONE. Therefore, mastering good obedience in the home can lead to practicing more difficult challenges in public on your journey to making your dog the most well-behaved version of himself that he can be.

Q What if other people interfere with my training?

Something that I see quite often is other people allowing someone else's pup to jump up on them. I was with my friend out in public with her puppy the other day when someone came up and started petting the pup. The puppy jumped up on the person, my friend told her puppy "OFF," and the other person said, "It's alright, I don't mind."

I see this all the time and it's really frustrating when you're the dog owner trying to enforce proper behavior. It makes correcting this behavior a lot more difficult when other people are allowing or encouraging your pup to do the opposite of what you are training him to do. In these situations, kindly inform the other person that you are working on training your dog NOT to jump up on people, and would like them to please not allow your pup to jump up on them.

❧ DESTRUCTIVE CHEWING:

You know well by now that dogs have a strong need to chew. Puppies don't know what is and what is not appropriate to chew on until you teach them. I know that it's SO easy to get frustrated with your pup for chewing on (and probably destroying) your favorite sandals or your brand new couch, so let's dive into this issue.

Q *Why do puppies feel the need to chew on everything?*

While you might think that your pup has set out to make your life a living hell, they actually have better reasons to chew than to simply add to your daily drama. There are a few key reasons for puppy chewing habits:

1. Puppies, like human babies, chew when they are teething; the chewing of objects soothes their gums.

2. Similar to infants, puppies put objects in their mouths to figure out what the object is, and what to do with it.

3. Chewing is an outlet for dogs to exert energy. Your dog may be chewing when he is bored or has energy to burn off.

4. Dogs have an instinctual need to chew!

Your dog *needs to* and is *going to* chew, no matter how old he is! However, the good news is that you CAN control *what* your pup chews on.

To do this, you simply have to teach your pup what is appropriate to chew on and what is not appropriate to chew on.

While a dog's need to chew is imperative to his health, if this need is not properly directed to appropriate chewing objects in the puppy stages, this natural tendency can turn into a truly detrimental behavioral problem when not properly monitored.

How does one go about stopping destructive chewing? Here's your plan of action:

1. Be sure that you have appropriate chewing objects available for your pup.

I have established that dogs have a need to chew and are going to chew no matter what.

Therefore, you need to provide them with chewing items that are appropriate for them to chew on.

There are a lot of different types of acceptable chewing items for dogs.

As I discussed earlier, chewing objects benefit the health of your puppy's teeth and gums and can provide your pup with healthy and essential minerals. (See The Puppy Preparation Checklist for a list of my approved chewing items)

2. Be very strict with what is appropriate to chew on and what is not.

Do not EVER let your pup chew on an inappropriate object—not even once... as with the rest of the training process, consistency is key to getting the results you want.

Your pup is still learning right from wrong, so you need to make sure that you are teaching him right from wrong in every area of his life, including what is right to chew on and what is not.

If you are repeatedly telling your puppy to not chew on an inappropriate object, at some point you may think that it is easier to just give up and allow your puppy to chew on the object.

Do not do this!

If you allow your pup to chew on an inappropriate object, even once, all the progress you had made to that point will be thrown out the window.

I know I sound like a broken record about this but raising a puppy is a series of repetitive actions performed over and over again!

It will get annoying having to repeat things a million times, but that is what you must do to have an excellent pup. With all of these methods, I'm pushing you to aim for 100% success, to do it right every single time. While that's probably not going to happen, if you're at 80 or 90% effectiveness in everything you do, you're going to end up with an incredibly well-behaved and well-trained pup. Whereas if you're only enforcing my methods HALF of the time, your pup won't even be 50% as good as what he could be. Your dog will match the standards you set for him so make sure you're aiming high!

The bottom line is you need to be consistent and strict with what is appropriate to chew on and what is not.

I promise that even if it seems as though your puppy will never learn to stop chewing on inappropriate objects, he WILL as long as you are consistent in guiding him.

3. Redirect your puppy to an appropriate object to chew on.

This is hands down the most important step!

If your puppy does try to chew on an inappropriate object, tell your puppy "No" and redirect him to the appropriate chewing object.

If you don't redirect your puppy's attention to an acceptable item, he will continue to find new objects to chew on to satisfy his urge.

Just as we talked about in the "mouthing" section, simply telling your puppy "No" will not teach him anything.

For example, let's say your puppy is chewing on your shoe and you tell him "No".

Why would your puppy, who has a need to chew, want to stop chewing on your shoe in that situation?

What motivation does "No" give him to stop?

If you were hungry, had food sitting in front of you, and someone told you "No, you can't eat that", what motivation would you have to stop?

Your pup may or may not stop chewing on your shoe at that point. If he *does*, this is where owners think: "Well, he listened so he must understand that shoes are not appropriate objects to chew on."

However, if your pup stops chewing, it's not because he actually understands that the shoe is an inappropriate chewing item. He will stop because he understands that Mom/Dad is mad and that he is in trouble! The second you leave the room, he will most likely resume chewing on that shoe because his need to chew is of course still present. It always will be.

Therefore, instead of just telling your puppy "No", you must REDIRECT him to an appropriate chewing item that will satisfy his need to chew.

Redirection is key to stopping destructive chewing and it is a step that most dog owners never take in their attempt to shape behavior.

So… yes, you WILL have to be persistent and consistently redirect your puppy to appropriate objects.

But, the more consistent and persistent you are, the faster your puppy will learn and stop those inappropriate chewing habits!

You should be monitoring your pup at all times, so there is no reason why you should always be finding already destroyed items. But, there will be the occasional thing you find chewed up and think: "How in the world did he get to this without me seeing it?!" Puppies are so sneaky sometimes!

But just as if you found a pile of poop in the house but didn't see your puppy making the mess, **you can't scold your pup when you find an item that he chewed previously.** If you catch your pup in the act, though, that is a different story.

To recap, if you catch your puppy chewing on an inappropriate item:

🐾 Tell him "NO."

🐾 Take the item away from your puppy (or your puppy away from the item).

🐾 Redirect your puppy to an appropriate chewing item (a toy or bone).

It's that simple. **If you catch your pup going for an inappropriate item, just redirect him to an appropriate one.** Keep in mind that it will take puppies a while to learn what he can chew, so be patient. Even if you are upset, remember to strictly follow these steps because excessively scolding your puppy is not going to do you any good.

Also remember to never put your pup in the crate as a punishment. You can absolutely put him in the crate to take a break, however, redirect him to his chew toy in the crate.

When you have your pup out of his crate, be cautious of what is on the floor or within his reach. Your puppy WILL try to get into WHATEVER he can. When you think that your pup would never touch something, it's fate that he will end up trying to chew it, so just remove the object from the equation to eliminate the possibility of a tragic ending for your new shoes.

The simplest advice I can give is this: **Don't leave things out that you don't want your puppy to get into and watch him like a hawk when he is out of his crate.** I always tell my clients: If you are not able to have both eyes on your puppy at all times, put him in his crate with a bone or a chew toy. Yes, puppy parenting is a full-time job!

❧ PULLING WHILE ON LEASH:

Pulling on the leash is a very common issue I come across with my clients. In fact, I see this issue ALL the time as I am just walking down the street! People seem to have a very hard time correcting this problem and tend to give up fairly quickly, allowing their dog to forever pull on the leash. The good news for you is that following my advice will keep your pup from pulling on the leash and you will no longer have to deal with the issue of your dog walking *you!*

Q *Is this really that big of an issue?*

I can't think of a reason why anyone would like to be pulled by his or her dog. You are walking your dog; he isn't walking you! Plus, **if you allow your pup to pull on the leash, he will do it forever. It's NOT something he will just grow out of as he gets older.** Also, as you should know by now, this kind of behavioral fix is something that is far easier to teach to puppies than it is to correct in adult dogs.

Once adult dogs are larger and stronger, it makes it considerably harder to teach them not to pull on the leash. It can also be very hard on your body if your dog is always pulling you. You may think it is not that big of a deal when your small puppy is pulling on the leash, but once he is stronger, you may feel differently.

Bottom line, the leash should *never* be tight while you are walking your pup!

Rather, **"loose leash" walking** is the gold standard. Loose leash walking means that there is always a little bit of slack in the leash between you and your puppy.

There are a number of reasons why you want your pup to walk on a loose leash instead of pulling:

🐕 You want your dog to respect you and know that you are the pack leader.

🐕 You don't want him to think that he leads you.

🐕 When a puppy pulls on the leash, it puts a lot of pressure and stress on his neck which can be very harmful to him.

🐕 Pulling can be damaging to the joints in your arms and shoulders.

🐕 Taking a dog for a walk with a loose leash provides for a much less stressful and more enjoyable walk while protecting your body and your puppy's health.

Q *What should I do if my puppy is pulling on the leash?*

🐕 Any time the leash tightens, stop right where you are.

🐕 When your pup looks back at you, tell him your clicker word.

🐕 Wait for your pup to come back toward you and reward him with a treat when he does.

🐕 If your pup isn't coming back towards you, lure him back to the heeling position with a treat.

🐕 If your pup *still* isn't coming to you, **take a step back and continue to do so until he does.**

🐕 Repeat the whole process again until your puppy understands how to walk on a loose leash.

🐕 Practice this routine until it becomes a habit for your pup.

Q *What if I'm barely making any forward progress while I'm training my pup to walk on a leash?*

Don't get discouraged if it seems as though you have to take a step back with every step forward you take. You may set out to do a walking training session and only make it half a block and that's okay!

I always tell my clients to not focus on distance but quality instead, when correcting or teaching proper leash walking manners.

Exercising your pup's mind will tire him out just like physical exercise does. Meanwhile, the more you can reinforce that your dog only gets to be walked when he is walking appropriately, the faster he will grasp the concept and not try to pull. Once again, it's putting in more work now for a lifetime of enjoyable walks!

Q *Is there anything I can use to make walking my pup easier?*

As I mentioned in The Puppy Preparation Checklist, **using a harness will IMMENSELY help keep your pup from pulling on the leash.** It is a fantastic tool, and I strongly recommend a harness to every dog owner. Not only does it help keep the dog from pulling on the leash, but it also removes all pressure and stress from the pup's neck. I have found that chest-led harnesses work the best for training your dog to have proper leash walking manners.

🐾 Not Wanting To Walk On A Leash:

Some people have the opposite problem of their pup pulling on the leash—their puppy doesn't want to walk on the leash at all! This is very common for young puppies who have no or little exposure to walking on a leash. However, most puppies will catch on to walking on a leash rather quickly, after a few times of introducing it.

If your puppy is stopping in his tracks and not wanting to walk on the leash:

- Pull on his leash gently to the side while telling him to "come."

- If that doesn't work, call him to you with a treat.

- **If neither of the above work, put a harness on your pup and repeat.**

- The great thing about using a harness is that you now have more control and the pressure is no longer on your puppy's neck. You can pull on a harnessed leash harder than you can when your puppy is only wearing a collar.

- **Once he walks to you, reward him with the clicker word and a treat.**

- If he is responding well to this, try calling him to you without a treat and just reward him with the clicker word.

- Repeat the whole process again until your puppy understands how to walk on a leash.

- Practice this routine until it becomes a habit for your pup.

Grizzly had this issue when I first brought him home. He would not follow me for a treat or *anything*. He completely froze when I would put a leash on him. However, as soon as I put a harness on him, it worked wonders.

Q *Why is the harness so effective?*

With a harness, you don't have to worry about applying too much pressure to your pup's neck by pulling on the leash, and you are able to pull on the leash with more force.

Some people run into this issue with older dogs, who are trying to control the walk. If you're experiencing this with your dog, you will want to use the leash walking exercise just described and practice daily to work through this stubborn behavior.

❧ UNCONTROLLABLE ROUGHHOUSING AND ZOOMING

Puppies tend to get into extremely crazy moods where they zoom around to the point where they essentially lose all self-control and may start behaving very rough. When a puppy is in this state, just redirecting him is usually not enough. The more excited a pup is, the further away he is from having total self-control and thus, the more excited he is, the harder it is for him to control himself at all.

The most effective way to work through these extreme spurts of energy is to try to gain control of it before your pup's energy escalates out of control.

It's very important, especially if you have kids, that nobody tries to get the pup riled up into this state. I strongly recommend teaching your kids to not run around and try to get the dog to chase after them. I know that it's super fun for kids to do this, but I recommend holding off on this until you teach your dog to control himself when he is excited.

I have seen far too many clients go against this advice and end up with their pup terrorizing the kids by nipping and roughhousing them to the point where the kids become afraid of the pup!

Even if the kids really enjoy playing chase with your dog, I strongly suggest not allowing that in the beginning until you truly get a handle on the basic obedience. While I'm not going to tell any of you how you should parent your child, when it comes to raising an obedient pup, the bottom line is your dog will never learn the necessary self-control that he needs to be well-behaved if he is always being allowed to be uncontrollably stimulated as a pup.

So, when you see your pup's excitement building, the best way to gain control is to make him sit. Sitting forces your dog to calm down and have self-control.

If your dog is already in this state, remember that he has already lost self-control. I suggest diffusing the situation by removing him or you (and your kids) from the situation so that he doesn't exert this total loss of control onto you (or your kids).

Earlier I mentioned that redirection is likely not enough to stop this behavior. This is due to the fact that your dog has lost all sense of self-control and his mind is so overstimulated that it's difficult to grab his attention. However, *after* you've removed you or your dog from the situation that was causing the loss of control, I've found that the best way to redirect this behavior is to pick him up or leash him and redirect him to go outside to run and exert energy. If you do not have the luxury of a backyard to easily redirect him to, I would first put him in his crate to force him to calm down from this excited state. Once he has calmed down, take him outside to allow him to exert his energy in an appropriate manner.

❧ Separation Anxiety:

Separation anxiety refers to your dog getting upset or stressed when you leave him anywhere. **A dog that has separation anxiety may bark, howl, cry, pace, destroy objects, attempt to get out of his crate, or have accidents in the house.**

However, a lot of owners think that their dog has separation anxiety, when in actuality, the behaviors the dog is exhibiting are learned behaviors and not true separation anxiety. Rather, the dog has learned that if he acts badly, he will get attention.

Therefore, he will bark in the crate, destroy items, whine, etc. just to get the attention that he wants. It is very easy for me, as a behaviorist, to determine if the dog has true separation anxiety, or if the dog is just exhibiting these behaviors for attention.

If your dog truly has separation anxiety, he experiences emotional stress when you leave.

However, owners sometimes mistake their dog's barking (for attention or to get what he wants), as separation anxiety, when it actually is not.

Therefore, it's very important to understand the difference between real separation anxiety and learned behaviors because there is a different course of action to take if you are needing to correct your pup's learned behaviors.

Working through true separation anxiety in dogs is definitely something that takes time but it certainly is manageable when addressed with the correct approach.

Q *What causes separation anxiety in dogs?*

In my experience working with dogs, I have found that every case of separation anxiety is unique.

There is typically not one, concrete answer as to what causes the separation anxiety in each individual dog because there are a number of unique genetic and environmental factors which have contributed to the development of separation anxiety, and they vary between every dog.

Factors such as...

- What happened to the dog in his past?
- How long is he left alone each day?
- Was he crate trained properly, so that he associates the crate with positivity?
- How does the owner respond to his unwanted behaviors?

Some dogs are inherently more attached to their owners as puppies, and are therefore more prone to developing separation anxiety, while other dogs end up developing it later on in life.

Working through separation anxiety is a process that is unique and different for each dog, depending on the circumstances and behaviors of the dog.

Fully overcoming separation anxiety in your dog will most likely take the help of a professional dog trainer or behaviorist, but I will give some general advice that can help with the process if you want to try on your own!

There are a few mistakes that dog owners make that can contribute to separation anxiety:

1. Rewarding Unwanted Behaviors.

The most common reason why dogs develop learned behaviors (mistaken as separation anxiety) is typically because of owners who incorrectly reward unwanted behaviors.

In fact, owners often feed into these behaviors in their dogs without even knowing it.

Crazy, right?!

When your dog is crying or whining, do you ever ask him: "Ohhh Rover, what's the matter?"

When your dog is barking just for attention, do you ever give in and give him the attention he is looking for?

I can almost guarantee that just about every dog owner has been guilty of responding to these behaviors in this way at least a couple times.

Q *What's wrong with this?*

Well, when you respond to these kind of unwanted behaviors, you are telling your dog: "When you whine or bark, you will get my attention."

When you give them this attention that they're so desperately asking for (in the form of unwanted behavior), your dog is going to think: "When I whine or continuously bark at mom/dad, I get my way!"

Therefore, your dog will continue this behavior of whining and/or barking because your response to these behaviors is the reward.

I'm going to repeat this point because one really can't stress it enough… your response to these unwanted behaviors is essentially rewarding your dog for misbehaving, which will only cause it to occur more frequently.

After fully grasping that crucial point, let me offer a suggestion.

Instead of rewarding your dog for exhibiting these unwanted behaviors, reward your dog for wanted behaviors. Well, duh!!!

This sounds very simple, but is SO overlooked by most dog owners!! When your dog is simply sitting calmly next to you and behaving, THIS is when he should be rewarded.

Yes—reward your dog for doing absolutely nothing at all! Positive reinforcement is all about rewarding your dog for the behaviors you want repeated.

Of course, we all want our dogs to sit calmly next to us and have their focus on us all the time. Well, then you must TELL them and REWARD them when they are doing exactly this!

When you reward your dog for being calm and quiet, he will think: "When I am calm and quiet and focused on mom/dad, I get rewarded", and will continue to practice this behavior. It is as simple as that!

2. Overdoing Hellos And Goodbyes.

Another extremely common way that owners feed into their dog's separation anxiety is by making goodbyes and hellos a big deal.

When you get home, do you ever greet your dog very excitedly saying something like: "HI ROVER! OH HI ROVER! I MISSED YOU SO MUCH!!!!"

I know that you are probably just as excited to see your dog after a long day at work as he is to see you, but making it a huge deal when you are reunited IMMENSELY contributes to a dog's separation anxiety.

When you make arrivals and departures a grand event, this often creates emotional stress for your dog while you are away.

Therefore, if you want to teach your dog to remain calm and keep his cool, you will have to practice calmness at both of these times. Try to make your goodbyes and hellos feel less important to keep your pup calmer.

Acting as though hellos and goodbyes are not a big deal is one of the most important things you can do to work through your dog's separation anxiety.

Of course, you can still calmly say "hi" to your dog and give him love when you get home, but wait until he is calm and sitting before you do so.

3. Leaving Your Dog Alone In A Poorly Conditioned Environment.

Another very important aspect of working through a dog's separation anxiety is thinking about where you leave your dog when you are gone, and how you introduce that place to your dog.

Q *Do you leave your dog in the crate every day when you are gone for 8 hours at a time?*

For many people, the answer may be yes.

What really makes the difference is your answer to my next question:

Q *Is this the only time that you leave your dog in the crate?*

Or even more important: the other times that you place your dog in his crate, is it to let him relax, or to punish him?

If you were put in a small room every day for 8 hours at a time, what would you think about the room? Probably like a prison! However, imagine that you were forced to stay in this tiny room every time you made a mistake. How much more would this make you dread that room?

Now, let's say that you were put in that same room every day for 8 hours at a time; but instead of your other exposure to that room being for punishment, it was your place to eat delicious meals.

This is the power of operant conditioning, that is, how certain stimuli and specifically, positive reinforcement, can positively impact the emotional state of your dog when he is left alone for long periods of time.

Q *So what can I do?*

By this point, you should grasp the point that how you associate certain spaces (such as their crate) with dogs while you're present will greatly impact how they feel when you're gone.

If the only time that your dog is in his crate is when you leave him in there for 8+ hours, or even worse, when you punish him as well, he is going to associate the crate with nothing but suffering and being abandoned for long periods of time.

You obviously want your dog to like being in the crate and not associate it with the negativity of being alone.

Therefore, if the crate is the big issue, you will need to go back to the basics of crate training, but for now, I will touch on the basics of associating the crate with positivity.

NOTE: If your dog is left in an enclosed space instead of the crate, use the same approach that I am describing, just substitute the enclosed space in for crate.

Q *How do you associate the crate with positivity to work through separation anxiety?*

1. Feed your dog his meals in the crate.

Food equals positivity in a dog's mind (and in ours too, let's be honest), so associate the crate with meal time and this will help your dog enjoy his crate.

2. Give your dog chewing items in the crate.

Antlers, bully sticks, and frozen Kongs make great chewing items that dogs love!

Chewing items are a very positive way for dogs to exert their natural need to chew, so chewing items in the crate are an excellent way to keep your dog distracted, and his emotions at bay.

3. Give your dog treats when he is in the crate.

Treats are an obvious positive! So be sure to reward your dog when he is in the crate with treats, treats, treats.

4. Give your dog these items of positivity EVERY time he is in the crate!

On top of these quick tips, it is very important that you make your dog understand that the crate does not always equal being alone for long periods.

5. Only let your dog out of the crate when he is behaving. NEVER let him out when he is crying and asking for attention.

Similar to what we discussed in the crate training section, acknowledging your dog when he is crying will cause him to associate crying with getting what he wants. Then, when he is left alone and does not want to be alone, he will cry in an attempt to get what he wants, and the separation anxiety will have begun.

To prevent this type of anxiety, allow your dog to have breaks inside the crate WHEN YOU ARE HOME in addition to the times that you are gone.

Have your dog spend some time in the crate while you are home so that he isn't automatically associating the crate with being left alone.

This practice makes your dog realize that just because he is going into his crate and you are leaving, does not mean that you will be gone for 8 hours every time.

For instance, if you start by putting him in the crate for very short periods, such as when you are just going to get the mail, it will slowly condition him to grow comfortable with spending time in the crate.

As he starts to get used to the crate and being left alone for short periods, you can slowly increase the amount of time he is in the crate—when you are running errands, shopping, etc.

Obviously you may still have to go to work and leave him for long periods as well.

However, the idea is that he won't get himself worked up prior to you leaving and think that you will gone forever, every single time he has to go in the crate.

As one final reminder, separation anxiety is a long process that some owners need to work on over the entire span of their dog's life!

Don't let that discourage you though, as I've equipped you with the best of the best, the knowledge and techniques that I use every day with my own clients.

A major change in a dog's life can also be a trigger of separation anxiety. **Changes in owner, home, or routine are a few examples, and all three of those are in play when you bring your puppy home for the first time.**

So, separation anxiety can start developing the moment you walk through the door with your new pup. Remember, this is the most significant change your puppy will go through in his life! Your puppy will most likely be upset about the change in the beginning, especially if he has just been separated from his mother and littermates.

Q How can I prevent separation anxiety?

You can prevent separation anxiety by avoiding the mistakes I just described above and by following all of my guidelines in Section 2 regarding bringing your new puppy home. However, keep in mind that some puppies do have more attached personalities and may need extra socialization work to prevent the early onset of anxiety.

If you have a pup like this and you begin to notice symptoms of separation anxiety, I recommend bringing your puppy to a dog day care or having someone else walk and play with your pup on a consistent basis so that he can get TONS of socialization and realize that you aren't the only great thing in his world!

I have seen AMAZING results from dogs with separation anxiety just by using this strategy and simply bringing them to a dog daycare once a week. Dog daycares are so helpful because instead of being alone and anxious all day, the dogs are very preoccupied and are given the opportunity to socialize with other dogs and humans.

❧ FEARFULNESS:

If you have an extremely reserved pup who fears the world (or just fears unfamiliar things), sheltering him from anything he fears will only do him MORE harm. The key in cases of fearfulness is to expose your puppy to the things he's afraid of in a gradual and positive manner.

If your puppy is afraid of new things:

- **Expose your puppy very, VERY slowly to the thing(s) that he fears.**

- Start with a large distance between your pup and the object of his fear.

- Associate the object of his fear with positivity by adding in something that your puppy really LOVES to the situation.

- If your pup is very food-motivated, give him lots of treats when exposing him to the object.

- Slowly move him closer and closer to the object that he fears as he gets more comfortable at each distance.

  - "Slowly" varies in degree between every puppy, so keep your pup's uniqueness in mind as you practice this exercise.

  - If your puppy seems unstressed and comfortable, you may be able to approach the object of his fear in that same day.

  - For other puppies, you may only be able to move an *inch* closer each day.

- Repeat the whole process **again and again** until your puppy has overcome his fear(s).

Throughout this process, read your puppy's body language and demeanor, and know his signals. Remember the stress signals I discussed earlier in Section 2 under "Understanding Your Puppy" and "Stress Signals." **You NEVER want to push your puppy too far when he is stressed and uncomfortable.** Pushing your pup past his limits in this situation will only make his fear of that object worse.

Some puppies which you could call reserved are often nervous or fearful around people in the beginning. Puppies like these are just hesitant to trust people right away, while others have a reason to be scared. You don't know what exactly happened to your pup before you brought him home, especially if you adopted him from a shelter or a rescue. It could be that your puppy fears people because someone gave him a reason to do so.

Q *Why do dogs develop a fear of people?*

A puppy's fear of people can stem from being mistreated by humans previously. It breaks my heart when I come across a puppy that came from a situation like this. But, it also makes me eager to show him that people will give him nothing but love, and I love working hard to gain a fearful puppy's trust.

I once had a foster puppy who was deathly afraid of people after being left in a box in a ditch. I knew that whoever had him previously had definitely mistreated him. Some dogs, however, just have a skittish personality.

Q *What should I do if my dog is afraid of me?*

You have to be extremely patient with this process. It can be incredibly disheartening to get a new pup, only to find out that he is afraid of you. However, as I mentioned in the introduction, giving up in this situation is the worst thing you can do.

Here is the best way to gain your puppy's trust:

- ⏌ First off, you can't gain a dog's trust in one day—**it takes time**.

- ⏌ **Treats, treats, and more treats** will be your best plan of action.

- ⏌ Give your pup LOTS of treats and love.

After reading this, you may think, "Well that seems too simple." That's the thing: when a new dog owner realizes that their puppy is scared of them, they often overcomplicate it and take it personally, instead of taking the simple yet necessary steps to gain their trust.

Q *Since my pup is afraid of me, does that mean I can't train him?*

Definitely not. **Some owners with fearful puppies make the mistake of letting their pup get away with EVERYTHING because they don't want to scold him or make him more afraid.** Don't fall into that trap! You still need to train your puppy as much as any other puppy, but it is all about the approach in which you do this.

Puppies who are sensitive/fearful tend not to need much scolding when they are doing something wrong. A simple "No" will usually get their attention and then you can redirect them to something else. Keep in mind that these puppies *especially* don't respond well to yelling or any forms of negative reinforcement.

Q *What should I do if my pup is afraid of strangers?*

Reserved puppies sometimes are skeptical or even fearful of people they do not know. You MUST socialize your pup with new people for him to get over this fear! The best way to do this is to essentially train your pup to look at you first, and if you say someone is ok, then he does not have to be afraid.

Q *How do you do this?*

Well, it's fairly simple:

Have someone who your puppy doesn't know help you out and go through the following exercise.

- Start with your puppy far away from this person.

- Have the person stay still, and move your pup to the person.

- This is important because your pup can move towards the person at his own pace.

  - **Alternatively, when someone approaches your puppy, it seems more threatening to the pup.**

- Before moving a step closer, call your pup to look at you and give your puppy treats.

- This teaches your pup to look to you if he feels uncomfortable, instead of continuing to fixate on the threatening person, which can end up forcing a dog to get even more worked up.

- Watch your pup's body language, demeanor, and signals.

- If your puppy seems ready for the next step (once you are close enough), **instruct the person to give your puppy treats and to allow the puppy to sniff them.**

- If your pup appears to be too stressed, stop there and give him treats until he gets comfortable.

🐾 If he is too stressed at any point, move backwards until you can find a distance where he is comfortable again.

When it comes to the other person, the way they act is imperative to this training exercise. **The most common mistake people make is how they approach dogs, especially reserved ones.** You should approach a puppy very slowly and calmly, especially when reaching your hand toward him. Always let the puppy sniff you before you try to pet him. When petting a nervous dog, NEVER reach over his head as this can be interpreted as an aggressive advance.

To get your pup comfortable with other dogs, follow the guidelines described above as well as the process below:

🐾 Let your pup watch other dogs from a distance for a while.

🐾 Let your puppy watch those dogs play and have fun.

🐾 Gradually, bring him closer to the other dogs.

🐾 Keep in mind that you will probably have to stay in one spot a lot longer than with a person until your dog is calm.

🐾 When you are first introducing your pup to other dogs, make sure the other dog is calmed and well socialized.

🐾 The last thing you want is a dog that will approach your puppy in the wrong way.

> Keep in mind that these guidelines are for pups that are just timid and need to be introduced to their new world properly, NOT for dogs who have developed a strong fear that could turn into aggression in certain situations. For dogs that I just described, see the section on reactivity.

🐾 BOLTING AND ESCAPING:

Hopefully, you are reading this before your puppy has successfully escaped out of the house. Obviously, having your puppy escape and possibly get lost is a traumatic experience for a family, but additionally, **once a puppy escapes out of the house, he is going to try even harder to keep doing it**.

Q *Why would my puppy want to escape? Is it because he doesn't like me?*

When a pup escapes, he gets the chance to roam freely, get into things, and do whatever he desires to do—everything a dog could dream of!

Escaping is a self-rewarding behavior for a dog, and because of this, it's a challenging one to break if your pup has already done it. So, the most important key to training a puppy not to bolt is to do everything you can to prevent him from doing it in the first place.

To prevent a dog from bolting or escaping:

- Be aware of where the dog is every time you are about to go out the door and make sure everyone in the house (including visitors) is aware of and adheres to this rule.

- Training a dog to sit and consistently wait before going outside can be extremely useful in this situation as well.

- If your yard is fenced, make sure it is very secure in every place—that there is no place where your pup could possibly squeeze through.

- **Make sure your pup is always on a leash if your yard is not fenced in.**

The last point is VERY important. Often, owners will allow their pup off the leash because "he has been really good about not escaping lately." **Don't even give your pup the opportunity to escape.** Be consistent with keeping him on a leash and teaching him his boundaries.

Q *Are there any other reasons why my puppy would try to escape?*

Sometimes, dogs try to escape because their needs are not being met at home. Dogs will try and escape for the following reasons:

🐾 Need for socialization

> 🐾 Make sure your pup is getting enough socialization with other dogs to prevent him from wanting to get out and find other dogs to play with.

🐾 Lack of exercise

> 🐾 Be sure that your puppy is getting enough exercise so that he doesn't go stir-crazy! A puppy that has a lot of energy who is cooped up at home is MUCH more likely to try to escape than a tired one who gets exercise.

🐾 Boredom

> 🐾 Often puppies want to escape just for the simple fact that they are bored and want to find something to entertain them. Make sure that your puppy has enough toys and entertainment to keep busy so that he doesn't yearn to go exploring for more.

🐾 To find a mate

> 🐾 This is a huge issue among un-neutered males. Fixing your pup will GREATLY reduce his attempts at trying to escape.

As a dog owner it's important to understand not just HOW to solve an unwanted behavior but also WHY your dog is exhibiting that behavior! In the meantime, here's how you can you prevent your dog from bolting altogether: Work on a "sit" and "wait" every time you go out the door with your dog. This teaches him that he doesn't have approval to leave and go on a walk, go play, etc until you have "released" him from the wait!

Another preventative tip is to work on strong recall both on and off leash so that if he ever gets out, you can feel confident that he will come when called.

In order to get to this point where you are more motivating than his reason to bolt (which is not easy, by any means), it will take a lot of recall practice on and off leash using treats to the point where he comes INSTANTLY every time you tell him to "Come".

If you're going to start working on this, PLEASE don't underestimate the difficulty of the process!

Your dog is rarely going to stop bolting on the first day you start practicing, so make sure you're not trying this out in the open when you first start out.

So... utilize enclosed spaces and start out small.

As you see improvement, grant more and more freedom until you're confident to test him out in an open space.

🐾 COPROPHAGY (EATING POOP):

Also known as "poop eating," coprophagy in puppies is more common than you may think. When it comes to puppies, they will most likely stand at one end of two extremes, that is, they'll constantly try to eat poop, or never try at all.

Whether it's his or other dogs' poop, puppies may eat poop for a few different reasons. **The most common reason for a pup to be practicing coprophagy is due to a lack of nutrition in his diet.** (Yet another reason why feeding your pup a high-quality, highly nutritious puppy food is so important!) If your pup isn't receiving the proper nutrients to meet his needs, he may try to find them elsewhere, and by "elsewhere" I mean in feces. Yuck!

If, however, you are feeding your pup a well-balanced diet and he's STILL trying to eat poop, then other factors could be causing this behavior.

The behavior could have started when he was a very young puppy, not yet weaned from his mother. How, you may ask? Well, when a mother dog has a litter of puppies, she often licks their feces to clean up after the pups. **When the puppies see their mother doing this, they may copy her actions and begin coprophagia.**

Other factors that could induce coprophagy include:

- Boredom
- Stress
- Anxiety

Q *What should I do if my puppy is eating poop?*

As in all unwanted behaviors, prevention is the best possible way to keep a dog from eating his own poop. **Just like when a dog escapes, coprophagia is a self-rewarding behavior, meaning that once a dog does eat feces and likes it, he will continue to attempt this behavior.** However, if you do find yourself in the situation where your pup is drawn to eating poop, here is a proven method that I have used to eliminate this habit:

- Always go outside with your pup, and don't let him go near feces.

- Even if you think your dog is just trying to smell it, there's no need for a dog to be sticking his nose in a pile of poop.

- Sniffing the poop just makes the chances higher that your puppy will try to eat it, so don't even let him go near it in the first place.

- When you see your dog interested in or going near the poop, **use the command "Leave It".**

If your puppy doesn't know the command yet, **still make sure to say it and then get him away from the poop in whatever way you can, and then reward him with a treat.**

- Whether it be picking him up, chasing him away from the poop, or getting him to come to you, any way you can get him away from the feces will be sufficient.

- Practice this consistently until your pup no longer exhibits this behavior.

❧ EXCESSIVE BARKING & WHINING:

Excessive barking can be one of the most frustrating behavioral issues you come across as a new puppy owner. In my experience, this problem can also be one of the biggest stressors in a dog owner's relationship with their pup, which is why it's so incredibly important to solve it before it gets to a seemingly uncontrollable level.

Dogs usually begin to bark excessively for the following reasons:

- **To gain your attention**
- **To assert dominance over animals or passersby**
- **Out of fear or uncertainty**

Q *What should I do if my pup is excessively barking?*

To accurately answer that question, **you need to identify whom or what your puppy is barking at, and more importantly,** *why.*

·············· *If your puppy barks at YOU:* ··············

If your puppy is barking at you, he is almost certainly doing it for attention and/or control. Whether it's due to a lack of exercise or a need to be with the rest of the 'pack' so to speak, this behavior needs to be corrected immediately.

Here is a step-by-step method to follow in order to correct this issue:

- If your pup continues to bark, **turn your back on your pup and ignore him until he stops barking.**

- He might continue to bark for a long time, so you must be patient!

- **Once he stops, give him a lot of attention, praise,** *and/or* **treats.**

- Repeat the whole process any time your puppy barks at you until he stops using it as a means to gain your attention.

🐕 If your pup will not stop, give him a break in the crate and repeat until he stops barking.

········· *If your pup barks at animals and/or passersby:*·········

This issue can be not only embarrassing for you when bringing your pup out in public but also frightening to strangers who don't know your dog and whether he's friendly or dangerous.

In my experience, **one of the biggest requests I get is teaching their dog to be able to go out in public and refrain from barking at other dogs.** If this is one of the goals at the top of puppy parenthood goals that you set in "Introduction To a Better Life With Your Puppy," then focus up and prepare to implement the process described below.

The typical scenario that I see when a dog is barking at another dog is this:

The owner screaming "Rover, No! Stop! No!!"

And then the dog continues to bark. Well, what motivation are you giving your dog to stop barking? Someone yelling "No" at me sure wouldn't be motivating to me!

You have to shift how you respond to your dog's barking first!

When your pup is barking while looking at dogs or people through a window:

🐕 Call his name positively to focus on you instead.

🐕 The "positively" aspect of this is the most important and also the hardest. You have to be more motivating than what your pup is distracted by, which is no easy task!

🐕 Once he looks at you, reward him.

Refocus his attention onto something else, such as a toy or bone, or try to keep his mind busy with training commands and treats.

If your pup is barking at objects, dogs, or people while out on a walk, he is either barking out of fear or over-excitement. To fix this, you must associate the trigger of what is causing him to bark with positivity and, at the same time, teach him how to to have self-control.

When your pup is barking at animals or people while out in public:

🐾 If your pup is already barking, move far enough away from the stimuli so that he isn't barking at it.

- If you are aware of stimuli that may cause your pup to bark, start far enough away so that he **doesn't begin** to bark at it.

🐾 When he looks in the direction of the stimuli, call his name to redirect his focus back onto you and give him a treat.

★ This is to help him associate that stimulus with positivity.

🐾 As your dog calms down and gains self-control, slowly move closer to the stimuli.

★ With each step, it is important that you redirect him back to you, and make him gain total self-control (commanding him to sit and lay down is the best way to do this) and comfort before moving forward.

- The degree of slowness varies between dogs, and can take days or weeks to actually get all the way next to the stimuli.

🐾 **Make sure you maintain control and ensure that your pup is relaxed throughout the process.**

🐾 If your dog starts barking at any point, move further away and refocus his attention on you.

As with any other training exercise, stay calm when trying to get your pup to stop barking. Yelling will only add to the madness of his barking, and he may think you are trying to bark along with him. As with all training aspects, you must be very consistent. **Don't EVER allow him to bark excessively.** If he gets away with it once, he will continue to think it's an appropriate behavior to perform.

Q *Why does my dog whine excessively?*

I come across this issue very often with my clients. I have a client whose one-year-old Frenchie pup was whining every 5 minutes—all day, every day. My client asked what she is doing wrong and why her dog is not happy. [Keep in mind that her dog is extremely well taken care of, exercised, well-fed, and her needs are being fulfilled every single day].

I told her this: There is absolutely nothing that she is doing wrong and that her dog's whining is a learned behavior.

If your dog is constantly whining, it is because you have been giving him attention when he whines and feeding into the whining behavior. Every dog owner has probably been at fault of this at some point-when your dog whines, you feel bad and ask him "What's wrong Rover? Why are you crying?" This attention that you are giving him for the whining is feeding into this behavior.

Q *So how do I stop the whining?*

There is just one step to solving this behavior:

Ignore your dog when he is whining!

Giving your dog what he wants when he is crying reinforces the whining behavior. Ignoring him when he is whining shows him that he does not get what he wants when he is whining.

Reward him when he is calm and quiet and your pup will stop this learned behavior!

❧ BEING ON FURNITURE:

Q *Is it okay if my puppy jumps up on the furniture?*

This is a question I get from clients frequently. This is one of the only questions where my answer is: "It's up to you." Allowing a puppy to be on the furniture isn't going to make him a misbehaved pup. A spoiled one, yes, but it will not affect his behavior in other areas.

However, if you don't want your pup on the furniture, it is completely understandable, and I'm happy to help. **Whatever you decide, be firm with your decision. This means that you can't allow your pup on the furniture sometimes and then other times scold him for being on it.** I know I always say it but this will only confuse your puppy, so decide which way you want to go with it and stick to that.

If you don't want your pup on the furniture:

- **Be strict from the start and NEVER allow him on the furniture.**

- If he jumps up onto it, tell him "OFF."

- **Motivate him to get off the furniture and onto the floor by drawing him down with a toy or treat.**

  - If he isn't getting off that way, it's alright to guide him down by his collar.

- Reward him when he does get off the furniture with the clicker word and praise/treat.

Prevention is the best way to work through any behavior! If you ever see your dog going for the couch, automatically direct him to sit and reward him for sitting on the floor. It is important to show him that he gets attention for the appropriate behavior.

🐾 Digging:

This behavior isn't necessarily detrimental to a puppy's overall behavior; rather, it's really just harmful to the owner's yard or wherever your puppy likes to dig.

If you don't mind your yard being covered with massive holes everywhere, then be my guest and allow your pup to continue this behavior. However, most people find digging to be very annoying and difficult to overcome.

Reasons why dogs dig:

🐾 Because they are bored.

🐾 They are using it as a means to exert energy.

🐾 It's in their genetics (due to their breed).

Q *How can I prevent my dog from digging?*

As I've reiterated throughout this handbook, **if your dog isn't being entertained or exercised properly, he will find his ways to entertain himself and exert energy.** Usually, these ways are less than ideal.

Therefore, if you're properly stimulating and exercising your pup, you shouldn't have this issue. A puppy who is exerting his energy into playing with his toys, chewing on bones, and getting enough exercise will not find the need to dig holes in the yard.

If, however, it's in your pup's genetics to be a digger, there aren't any preventative measures you can take. **You just have to correct the behavior when you see your dog digging.** Therefore, in order to stop this behavior, you must be watching your pup at all times when he's in the yard.

If you catch your dog digging:

🐕 If you catch your pup in the act, **tell him "NO" firmly and get him away from the hole.**

Immediately redirect him to an appropriate item he can exert his energy into, such as chewing on a bone or running laps around the yard.

🐕 If you find a new hole that you didn't see your puppy digging, there's nothing you can do to correct that behavior.

- Remember, you can't discipline your puppy for a misbehavior you didn't catch him doing.

  ★ Your pup doesn't remember that he dug that hole one minute ago. Scolding him at this point will do no good, as your pup will not understand what you are scolding him for.

❧ BEGGING:

If you don't want your dog begging at the table, don't feed him from the table. It's as simple as that. You and everyone in your home must be very strict with the rule if you are going to enforce it.

If you think it is okay to occasionally slip your pup food from the table but do not want him begging, you are contradicting the situation. **This lack of discipline and consistency is often why so many dog owners have this issue.** Dogs are extremely intelligent. They always seem to remember that one time they were given food from the table, and will try to see what they can get away with from then on.

Once again, the solution to this problem is very simple:

🐾 **Put your pup in the crate during mealtime, EVERY time.**

- Removing your puppy from the situation so that he doesn't feel tempted is the best way to handle begging.

- Once he learns that your mealtime is not time for handouts and he is able to have more self control around food, you can direct him to his bed or a different spot while you eat.

🐾 **If you do want to give your pup table scraps, just don't feed him from the table!**

- Instead, put him in his crate while you enjoy your meal and then give him the scraps in his bowl inside the crate.

🐾 Mounting:

Mounting (the polite term for "humping") is a behavior that many dog owners will come across with a new pup. However, you should never allow your dog to mount other dogs (or people). Even if it is just playful, it isn't appropriate behavior.

Some people think it's funny when their dog mounts other dogs, but it is a behavior that needs to be discouraged. Why? **If your dog mounts a dog who doesn't like it, the situation can turn aggressive very fast.** Also, mounting is a behavior, along with jumping, that can make other people angry and/or uncomfortable.

A lot of people think that only male dogs are capable of mounting other dogs, which isn't true at all. While it's more common in males, females perform mounting as well.

Q *Why do dogs mount?*

- **To initiate play**
- **To assert dominance**
- **As a sexual behavior**

Q *How do I stop my dog from mounting people and other dogs?*

🐾 Get your pup fixed!

- Neutering or spaying your puppy will help IMMENSELY in getting your pup to stop this inappropriate behavior.

🐾 Mounting is also behavior that is often preceded by other behaviors that foreshadow it.

- **Before a dog mounts another dog, he usually will act like he is obsessed with the dog: sniffing him and not leaving him alone.**

Then, he will attempt to jump up on the other dog or wrap his paws around its torso.

🐾 **If you see these behaviors or your dog starts mounting, remove your dog from the situation.**

Mounting is an obsessive behavior, so I can almost guarantee that your dog will not zone out of it on his own and will most likely keep trying to mount the dog as long as he is around him so you will have to start the redirection by physically redirecting him away from the dog he is obsessing over.

🐾 Be consistent! Never allow your dog to mount another dog, even if the other dog's owner says it's alright.

> *It is important to stop and redirect this behavior to appropriate play immediately. People often laugh and think it is hilarious when their puppy mounts, but when it turns into an obsessive behavior it suddenly isn't so funny anymore. Correct and redirect this behavior the FIRST time you see your dog exhibiting it.

🐾 Playing Too Rough:

Many first-time dog owners do not know what type of play is appropriate between dogs and what isn't. I find that people either allow their pup to get away with play that is too rough and inappropriate or they get overly protective about puppy play that is completely normal.

This is a very fine line to negotiate, so be sure you know these boundaries. **Keep in mind that puppies need to play with other dogs to get proper socialization and develop into well-rounded pups, so allowing acceptable puppy play is very crucial to your pup's development.**

Q *What is appropriate puppy play?*

🐕 Mouthing one another

- Puppies play with their mouths and often what looks mean, really is completely normal for puppies.

- **Be sure your puppy is playing with his mouth gently and isn't latching onto the other dog or biting down hard.**

- All puppies partaking in the fun should be relaxed.

- All puppies that may be playing together should have relaxed facial expressions and demonstrate self-control.

🐕 Barking or growling noises

- Puppies will be a little bit noisy when playing and sometimes will make quiet growling noises.

- However, if the noises get too loud or sound more aggressive, the play should be broken up.

🐾 Play bowing

- Play bowing is when a dog leans his front legs down to the floor and sticks his butt up in the air. This is a playful move and tells the other dog "I am ready to play."

Q *What type of puppy play is inappropriate?*

🐾 Neck Biting

- **Dogs should NEVER bite each other's necks!**

  ★ Keep your pup from biting other dogs' necks, even if it appears to be a gentle bite.

  ★ The reason for this is because the jugular vein is located in the neck. **If a jugular vein is punctured, it can be fatal.**

🐾 Lack of self-control

- This can be anything from knocking other dogs over when unaware of their surroundings or harassing other pups that don't want to play.

Often times, pups lack self-control when they get too excited and then the behavior crosses over the line to being inappropriate. To keep it from getting to this point, it's really good to break up puppy play every so often even if they are playing appropriately, just to keep them from getting over-stimulated.

🐾 HERDING OTHER DOGS OR PEOPLE:

Q *What should I do if my pup is herding other dogs or people?*

Some dogs have been bred specifically for herding, so this is a behavior that takes time to correct. As with all of the behavioral problems I've discussed throughout this book, **the best way to remedy this behavior is to prevent it from manifesting in the first place!** While I understand that it seems I'm being redundant when it comes to this point, many new dog owners don't realize how much control they have over the way in which their puppy behaves!

With that being said, refrain from putting your pup in situations where he's able to herd. Why should you do this? Herding is genetically bred in some dogs, and they don't have the self-control to stop themselves from doing it. If your pup is in a place where he would possibly have an urge to herd—anywhere dogs or people are running around—you should keep him on the leash. Prevention is key. Do NOT even give him the opportunity to herd. Once he learns to have better self-control, focus, and recall back to you, you can slowly work your way to letting him off the leash in these environments.

I understand that there may be times where you can't always prevent your pup from herding. However, here are a few ways that you can put yourself in the best position to correct this behavior:

🐕 **Learn your pup's foreshadowing signal.**

- Usually, herders will foreshadow herding with behavior such as crouching down or fixating on the person/dog they want to herd.

🐕 If you see him indicating his signal, call him to you with a treat to prevent him from going through with herding.

❧ **If he doesn't come to you and goes on to herd, tell him "NO," leash him, and remove him from the situation.**

❧ Repeat the whole process any time your pup exhibits these behaviors or begins herding until your puppy stops attempting to herd.

The best way to break this natural instinct is to practice with him on the leash so that he cannot ever go through with the herding behavior. Call him to you when he starts to exhibit his foreshadowing behaviors and be patient. He will eventually come back to focusing on you. When he does so, reward him. The amount of time it takes him to snap out of that zoning in on the object will get shorter and shorter the more you practice.

This is a behavior pattern that is tough to break, so be patient because it may take a long time to correct.

🐾 REACTIVITY:

With both reactivity and aggression, the issues are complex and unique to each individual dog. I strongly suggest that you consult a trainer/behaviorist to help determine the best way to work through the reactivity you are experiencing with your dog.

Reactivity is very often mistaken for aggression, so it is important that you first understand the distinction. People often call me and tell me: "My dog is aggressive on the leash. He constantly barks at other dogs going by, but once he gets to meet the dog, he is completely fine and friendly."

If your dog is friendly once he gets up to the other dog, this is not aggression, it is reactivity.

Reactivity is simply when a dog is reacting to a situation. Typically, the dog reacts by barking and/or pulling on the leash.

The first step in working through reactivity is identifying the reason behind your dog's reactivity. For example, if you suspect that your dog has fear based reactivity, try to think of the possibilities which could have triggered this behavior.

Was he rescued from an abusive home?

Was he attacked by another dog when he was younger?

Was he not socialized well as a puppy?

These are all the kind of questions that you should be asking yourself. If you are aware of WHY your dog started exhibiting this behavior, then your training protocol to solve it will be much more accurate.

Reactivity is typically the result of a few different situations:

1. **The dog sees the stimulus (person, dog, etc.) as a positive thing and reacts because he is over-excited and does not know how to control himself.**

This type of reactivity happens when a dog associates the trigger of his reactivity as a positive thing and is so excited to see the person/dog that he loses all control. This loss of self-control results in barking and going crazy. I usually see this behavior in dogs who get along great with other dogs and people but need more self-control training.

This typically happens when owners continue to allow the dog to greet a person/dog even when he is in this over-excited (reactive) state. If the dog is never forced to control himself when he is extremely excited, then why would he do it on his own?

To work through this type of reactivity, you must work on self-control exercises with your dog, especially when he is excited. Whenever your dog is excited to see a person/dog, make him refocus his attention back to you and then direct him to sit. Once he is sitting or lying down and focusing on you, he can move forward. This may take some time for your dog to settle down and gain some self-control so be patient! Each time that you make him control himself before a greeting, the faster you will be able to work through this reactivity (and the more polite the greetings will be!)

2. **The dog sees the stimulus as a negative thing and reacts as a warning signal to show that he is feeling uncomfortable or threatened.**

This type of reactivity can be triggered when a dog associates the stimulus as a negative thing and is so fearful or scared to see the stimulus that he begins barking and/or lunging uncontrollably. I usually see this behavior in dogs who are fearful and/or nippy around other dogs/people and have experienced emotional trauma in the past.

While the causes of this form of reactivity differ among dogs, it is most likely that the reactivity is due to environmental factors such as a traumatic experience in your dog's life or a lack of socialization. Just as in humans, some dogs are more sensitive to traumatic experiences and social events than others, and therefore the triggers of fear based reactivity depend on the individual dog. As one example, your dog may associate a dog with negativity and react due to a negative experience with a dog in the past in which he was attacked. On the other hand, your dog may have developed fear based reactivity because his prior owner didn't take him out of the house until he was 6 months old, and now he is fearful of the entire world due to lack of exposure more most of his puppy hood.

This behavioral issue must be solved through the same processes of desensitization and counter conditioning described in the first type of reactivity. While the forms of reactivity described here differ in their triggers and sometimes their behavioral symptoms, the desensitization process remains the same. The goal of these processes are to display a behavior that is different than his current reaction to a stimulus. I will go into more detail about these processes below to provide clarity on how the processes are used.

3. **The dog is confused and reacts because he is unsure if the stimulus is positive or negative.**

The trigger for this type of reactivity is typically the same as in dogs who exhibit fear based reactivity. The difference between dogs who are confused and those who cross the line into fear based reactivity is based upon the point raised above: every dog is unique and responds differently to environmental factors. I typically see this behavior in dogs who are unsure around other dogs/people.

This type of reactivity must be solved through the desensitization and counter conditioning processes. The goal of these processes is to associate the stimulus with positivity instead of confusion.

Obviously, the lines can seem meshed at times between the different forms of reactivity, which makes reactivity an incredibly difficult behavioral issue to work through for dog owners around the world.

Even further, the solution processes of desensitization and counter conditioning can seem confusing at times, so here is a simple explanation of what the process entails:

Counter conditioning means training a dog to display a behavior that is different than his current reaction to a stimulus. Desensitization is the process of exposing the dog to a stimulus beginning at a very low intensity. Counter conditioning and desensitization need to be used together to be effective and are often used to change unwanted behavior in dogs, especially fearful and aggressive behaviors.

How to use counter conditioning and desensitization with your dog:

1. Be Aware

Think of instances in which your dog has reacted. Why is he reacting (excitement, fear or confusion) and what is causing him to react? For example, if your dog is afraid of people, you want to figure out exactly what he's scared of. Is he more afraid of adults than children? More afraid of men than women? More afraid of a family member or someone he doesn't know?

Some common factors to consider include location, loudness, speed of movement, distance, amount of time near the other animal or person and body language of the animal or person who induces reactivity.

2. Begin Where Your Dog Is Least Likely To React And Slowly Increase The Difficulty

The training should start in a location where the reactivity will not occur. For example, if your dog is fearful of another dog, start at a distance where he will not react. Whether this is five yards or 50 yards, you need to start at a location where your dog doesn't react. Find this sweet spot and gradually begin working closer to the stimuli.

3. Continually Associate The Situation With Positivity

Help your dog associate good things with the situation rather than negative things. This can be food (especially your dog's favorite treats), toys, and social reinforcements like petting, attention, and praise. If food is used it should be in very small pieces and be highly desired by your pet (such as hot dogs, cheese or high value treats). You may need to experiment a little to see what is the best motivator for your pup.

4. Don't Move Closer Until Your Dog Is Calm And Ready To Advance

Dog owners always want to know how long they need to stay at a distance/intensity level before moving forward. This will depend completely on your dog, who should be demonstrating that he is associating the situation with positivity. This means that the dog is looking to me and focused on me or the treat instead of the stimulus—in contrast to his previous reactions such as barking, trembling or other fearful responses.

5. Take Your Time & Practice Consistently

Counter conditioning and desensitization take a LOT of time and should be done very gradually. Think through the steps you need to take. Rather than expecting progress in leaps and bounds, look for small, incremental change. It can be incredibly helpful to keep a log of your results, since day to day changes will likely not be big. As always, patient and consistent practice will be your best friend! Every dog will progress at his own pace and it's crucial that you're understanding of his unique learning capabilities. The only way you're going to get through this process successfully is by putting in a ton of work and staying optimistic throughout this long-term process.

Q *What is the difference between reactivity and aggression?*

Common signs of reactivity are lunging and extreme barking in response to different stimuli (other people and dogs, strange noises, even cars).

An aggressive dog is one that has exhibited the same behaviors of a reactive dog, but has crossed the very fine line between the two behaviors and tried or succeeded in biting a human or another animal.

Basically, the difference is this:

If your dog got the chance to get up to the person/dog he is reacting at, he is aggressive if he would attempt to bite the person/dog. If he would not attempt to bite the person/dog, he is only reactive.

When I am working with a reactive foster dog, I, being a behaviorist, never really know if the dog is actually aggressive when I first start working with him because I do not give him the opportunity to be aggressive. I immediately work through the reactivity and when doing this, I am also working through the possible aggression.

🐾 AGGRESSION:

As I just mentioned in the previous section, working through reactivity is often times the first step in working through aggression.

There are many types of aggression in dogs, each possessing its own set of challenges and hurdles to overcome when correcting behavior.

Many aggressive dogs are surrendered to high-kill shelters after incidents and need a long-term rehabilitation process, which I refer to as desensitization and counter conditioning.

The different types of aggression and reactivity you will come across are:

🐕 Territorial

- This behavior is due to your dog feeling the need to guard his territory.

  - ★ Whether it's your home, yard, or other environment, your pup doesn't want intruders in his space.

🐕 Protective

- This behavior is due to your pup feeling the need to protect you (his owner) or any human.

  - ★ He could also show this type of aggression when trying to protect other dogs.

🐕 Dominance

- Whether your dog is trying to assert dominance on a human or another dog, he will become aggressive when he doesn't want someone or another dog crossing a certain boundary or performing a certain action that your dog has associated as negative.

🐕 Fear/Defensive

- This behavior is the result of acting aggressive due to fear.

    ★ Dogs who fear that they are in danger, even when they usually aren't, will exhibit aggression to protect themselves.

    ★ This aggression typically stems from an incident in a dog's past that is essentially comparable to PTSD in humans.

🐕 Same-Sex

- This type of behavior is a lot more common than you might think and is tied to dominance aggression.

- Two females (or males) become aggressive with each other to establish dominance over the other member of the same sex.

🐕 Resource Guarding

- This type of aggression happens when a dog becomes possessive over his toy, food, etc. See the "Resource Guarding" section for more information.

    ★ When a dog or person comes near the object of his possession, he gets aggressive.

🐕 Prey Drive

- Some breeds are genetically wired to hunt small animals and have a high sense of "prey drive".

    ★ Dogs who have very high prey drive might go after smaller animals and become aggressive with them as if the animals are the dog's prey.

Q *What if my dog's type of aggression isn't listed here?*

As you attempt to diagnose your puppy's type of aggression, remember that these are just the most common examples I see in my work.

There are many others, with some that are unique only to individual dogs. Again, I strongly suggest that you schedule a one-on-one consultation with an expert trainer or behaviorist to diagnose your dog's specific needs.

Q *What should I do if my pup is being aggressive towards other dogs or people? How do I correct this behavior?*

The first step to correcting an aggressive or reactive dog is to understand if your dog is exhibiting truly aggressive or just reactive behaviors. If you haven't already, go back and read the section on reactivity to get an understanding of both behavioral issues

Now that you understand which type of behavior you're looking to address, there are different methods of correction for each type of aggression and reactivity, and every dog needs to go through a rehabilitation process at their own speed. If your pup is showing signs of aggression, I suggest to:

🐾 Determine what type of aggression your pup is exhibiting and what specifically drives him to be aggressive.

🐾 Keep your pup away from whatever is driving his aggression/ reactivity.

🐾 Be sure to keep your dog leashed when you are out anywhere, or someone is coming to your home so that you can control him.

🐾 If your puppy starts growling or shows other warning signs of aggression, **remove him from the situation immediately.**

🐾 Consult an expert trainer or behaviorist ASAP to work through your dog's individual unique aggression issues.

If you're looking to correct these behaviors on your own, I need to share some hard but necessary truths that you need to hear.

Overcoming reactivity and aggression are often very long-term processes which require identifying the specific stimuli that are setting off your dog, and then consistent, targeted work to help the dog shift their mental state.

The best way to help your dog work through these behaviors is by slowly conditioning them to see those stimuli as positive situations rather than continuing to associate them with the negativity that is causing them to act out. The depth and extent of this process is something that needs to be evaluated on a case by case basis and relies on factors such as your dog's age, past, relationship with you, genetics, past environment and many other determining factors that go beyond the scope of this book. For these reasons, if you have no experience working through these types of behavioral issues, the process can be very overwhelming as a dog owner.

The truth is, depending on the severity of your dog's case of reactivity or aggression, this is a behavior that may need to be worked through for the rest of your dog's life.... I know that is a tough one to hear but it's absolutely IMPERATIVE to have realistic expectations with the amount of time it takes to correctly work through behavioral problems (that is, getting to the root cause of their insecurity or past pain), especially reactivity and aggression.

The good news is, I've experienced many cases of severe aggression where I've been able to help owners work through in just a matter of weeks!

With that being said, regardless of where you believe your dog is at on the scale of severity, if your pup is being reactive or aggressive towards other dogs or people, once again, **I strongly advise you to schedule a one-on-one consultation with an expert trainer or behaviorist in your area.**

Reason being, these behaviors are not normal and will typically get worse without following an expert's advice. You want to fix this problem immediately while your pup is still young, or you may end up dealing with much larger consequences and a longer rehabilitation process later on.

🐾 RESOURCE GUARDING

Resource guarding is actually a relatively common canine behavior and is influenced by a number of environmental and situational stimuli, including a dog's natural instinct to survive.

For those who haven't experienced this behavior, resource guarding is a behavior exhibited by dogs that control access to food, objects, people and locations that are important to him through defensive body language or overtly aggressive behavior.

A resource guarder will not tolerate competition and will guard the resource to maintain priority access.

Guarding resources is usually a manifestation of the dog's deep-rooted insecurity and inability to cope well in a social situation, even with people and other dogs he knows.

An insecure dog can see anyone as a potential threat to a resource, whether that resource is food, toys, space, a mate or access to a particular person. The threat of losing the resource, and the good feeling that the resource provides makes a dog more angry and irritable.

This is where things may get tricky, as there are two main types of resource guarders: those that guard from humans, and those who guard from other dogs.

Resource Guarding From People

Typically, dogs that guard resources from people (often their owners) possess more deep-rooted issues that are more complex and difficult to overcome than when this behavior occurs toward another dog.

For that reason, if your dog is guarding resources from you or another person, I'd highly recommend consulting with a behaviorist in your area who can walk you through this process (similar to cases of aggression and reactivity) with your individual dog.

I will, however, give you a few exercises to help with this issue.

🐾 Feed your dog handfuls of kibble from your hand.

- This ultimately reinforces the saying: Don't bite the hand the feeds you!

🐾 When it is time to feed your dog, first set down an empty food bowl in front of your dog. Once your dog checks out the bowl and sees that there is nothing inside, pick it back up and put the food in it.

🐾 Teach your dog to "wait" for his food (you can learn how to do this in the command section)

Q   Should I Punish My Dog for Resource Guarding?

If you've read enough of my content, you know that I support only positive reinforcement training methods.

While there will always be those that object to positivity in every situation, I truly believe it is the only way to truly win over your dog and have a quality relationship with them; one where they want to listen to you and obey your commands.

With that being said, some people still misunderstand why their dogs guard and why there is social competition, therefore, many owners of resource guarders often get angry and confrontational with their dogs.

Confrontation, however, only increases competition in the dog's eyes and causes the dog to guard the contested resource even more. Using physical punishment on a resource guarding dog is the exact opposite of what you need to do.

Instead, make sure you understand your dog's situation and work to instill more confidence in him, so that he feels less threatened by your presence.

When working to rehabilitate a dog that aggressively guards his resources, he should not be forced into submission or physically punished!

It is much more effective to use counter conditioning to alter a dog's behavior... without your dog ever realizing that you are doing so! That, my friends, is the epitome of masterful dog training!!

................*Resource Guarding From Other Dogs*................

As with every misbehavior, prevention is key!

While prevention isn't helpful once the problem has begun, don't miss the chance to prevent resource guarding before it begins.

Say you have a new dog, Fluffy, and a long-term resident dog, Rover. You can teach Rover that a treat to Fluffy leads to a treat to Rover. And vice versa.

It's quite easy to do:

When you give a treat to one dog, immediately give the other dog a treat as well. Then reverse the order.

I'm doing this right now with my foster dog Riley. Every night after dinner all the dogs get a treat.

First, I make all of the dogs sit.

Then I'll say the name of one dog, perhaps Juneau and let her get some treats. Grizzly knows to wait his turn, but if Riley moves forward I move forward a step to block her, say "UH UH" to her, and redirect her to back to sit.

When she backs off, I'll then say her name to allow her some treats, then quickly say Grizzly's name and let him do the same. Then back to Juneau and all around about 3 or 4 times so that all the dogs learn that being patient and polite pays off!

I would never suggest doing this if you already have tension between your dogs. This is prevention, not a treatment. Think of this exercise as either the first step to prevent trouble when none yet exists, or the end game if you already have problems and are out of options.

Another factor to consider: the amount of excitement among the dogs during this exercise.

If the dogs begin to get excited and pushy, command them to sit and calm down. You want the dog to learn that being polite and patient gets the treat, not pushy and demanding.

Q What Do I Do if My Dog Is Already Guarding Resources?

1. In this case, I recommend to manage and avoid the situations that the resource guarding is occurring in until you are able to work with a dog trainer/behaviorist in your area that has experience working through these types of behaviors.

2. Determine in what situations the resource guarding is happening in. Is it over food? Any food or a certain kind? Inside, outside, on the bed? Try to find the root and be as specific as possible.

3. Prevent these situations from happening! Every instance that the food guarding does happen, it is a step backwards in working through the root cause.

    Feed the dogs in separate rooms, give treats in separate rooms, do whatever you can to prevent it while you work through the deep-rooted issue with your behaviorist.

4. Teach impulse control! This is an indirect way of handling the problem, but it definitely helps with the process.

    Dogs who resource guard are often dogs who cannot handle not getting what they want when they want it. Teaching self control is extremely beneficial for all dogs, especially ones who resource guard.

    Commands such as...

'Wait', 'Lay Down', 'Stay', and 'Leave It', are all great exercises to teach and practice self-control.

Your trainer should work with your dogs through a more direct process of desensitization and counter conditioning to treat the resource guarding.

The ultimate goal of this process is to take the trigger that is producing an unpleasant response in your dog's mind (and thus, making him feel the need to react and be aggressive), and replace it with positivity so that he feels confident and that the situation is positive, instead of negative.

This is a process that takes time and control to really work through, so do not feel discouraged if your dog's resource guarding is not solved after one session, or several for that matter!

Necessary Knowledge For The Most Dedicated Dog Owners

Congratulations! By making it this far into this comprehensive guide, you've demonstrated that you truly care about giving your pup the best life possible! In this last section, I'm going to give you the advanced knowledge that will put you ahead of the game not only for raising a happy puppy but a happy, adult dog, meanwhile saving you headaches and dollars in the process! Whether you're still preparing yourself for puppy parenthood or you've successfully implemented the earlier sections of this book, the information that follows gives you the invaluable knowledge that will complete this comprehensive puppy preparation guide. Therefore, get ready to apply this last section of necessary information to make you the best puppy parent possible!

🐾 SUCCESSFULLY SOCIALIZING YOUR PUP

Socialization is immensely important for your pup. Dogs have a need for socialization, just as we humans do. Therefore, your pup needs to be socialized with other dogs and people to be able to grow into a well-rounded adult. Everything you do with your pup during puppyhood shapes him into who he is going to be for the rest of his life. **If you keep your dog from socializing when he's a puppy, he won't develop the proper socialization skills he needs to interact with the world around him.**

KEYS TO SUCCESS

Socializing your pup is absolutely MANDATORY. Socialization is a fundamental piece of the puzzle in your puppy's healthy development into a well-trained member of your family.

Q *Why is socialization so important?*

Simply put, your puppy is going to be around other dogs for the rest of his life. Therefore, you want your dog to be able to interact with other dogs in a positive way. Your pup needs to learn the appropriate ways to greet, play, and interact with other dogs to be a well-rounded pup. **Socializing your puppy is also an excellent opportunity to observe his behaviors so that you can pick up on any potential behavioral problems sprouting up before they become an issue.**

Q *When should I start socializing my puppy with other dogs?*

This is where dog trainers and veterinarians sometimes clash heads. Vets will typically tell you that you need to wait until your puppy is fully vaccinated to socialize him with other dogs. This means that your dog will not be able to meet other dogs until he is about 5 months old. (Refer to the end of this section for more information on what vaccinations your puppy needs.) I do agree that you should not bring your pup to highly populated dog areas, like the dog park or dog beach, where his chance of contracting something is higher, until he is fully vaccinated. But, if your dog does not meet another dog until he is 5 months old, he is missing out on crucial socialization as part of his development and therefore is much more likely to develop behavioral issues.

Right now, I am working with a 6-month-old Golden Retriever pup whose parents followed their Vet's strict advice and did not take her out of the house until she was fully vaccinated at 5 months old. Since the only world the pup has ever known is inside of her house and her backyard, she is completely terrified of the outside world and other dogs. Now, at 6 months old, we are having to do an intense desensitization process to get her over her fears.

To avoid this, I strongly suggest that you introduce your pup to new situations once he has gotten his first round of shots. It is important that your dog is introduced to the outside world in a positive way. Obviously, you need to be cautious of where you are and what your pup could potentially be exposed to. I love to take my foster pups with me to TJ Maxx and have them ride around in the cart! This way, they are being exposed to people and new environments.

As far as being introduced to other dogs, I recommend waiting until your pup has his second round of shots. If, however, you want to get started on the socialization process before he is fully vaccinated, you want to make sure that you are only introducing your pup to dogs that you know and who are 100% healthy. One-on-one introductions with other dogs that you know is a great way to socialize in the beginning to ensure your pup's health and make sure that he is not too overwhelmed with the meeting.

Q *What if I don't have the time to socialize my puppy?*

In response to this question, I usually I tell my clients that they need to MAKE the time to socialize their pup. Not only is socializing fundamental to your puppy's healthy development into a well-behaved member of your family, but you have also made a very serious commitment to give your dog the best life possible. With that being said, if there is NO possible way for you to take the time to socialize your puppy, I strongly suggest looking into a dog daycare. I worked at a dog daycare throughout college and it was amazing for socialization. Juneau basically grew up there and developed into one of the most well socialized dogs I know—but I may be biased ;)

Find a dog daycare that cares about each dog individually, has structure, and enforces rules. There are some that give pups too much freedom and allow inappropriate play, so just be smart when choosing the right one for your pup. I have seen MANY dogs turn into well-socialized dogs just by going to dog daycare once a week. Not only is it great socialization for your puppy, but he will also come home super tired from a full day of playing! It's a win-win situation.

BRIGHT IDEAS

If you don't have enough time in your busy schedule to socialize your pup, consider taking him to a dog daycare weekly so that he can socialize with other dogs.

Q *What about socializing my puppy with other people? Isn't that important as well?*

Yes, socializing your puppy with other people is a very important part of raising a well-behaved dog. Socializing your pup with other people can help to prevent separation anxiety, reduce a puppy's nervousness or fearfulness, and help fulfill his socialization need. You want your pup to be friendly towards other people and exposed to as many different people as possible.

KEYS TO SUCCESS

Don't forget to socialize your puppy with people as well! Socializing your pup with new people can help to prevent separation anxiety, reduce a puppy's nervousness or fearfulness, and help fulfill his socialization need.

🐾 GROOMING 101

One of the biggest and most costly misconceptions when it comes to raising a puppy is in regards to grooming and the significant investment it requires on the owner's part.

From my experience, I have observed that my clients usually fall into one of two problem areas when it comes to grooming:

1. **They ignore grooming COMPLETELY.**

2. **They instill FEAR into their puppy when grooming due to a lack of knowledge and grooming protocol.**

············ *Those who ignore grooming COMPLETELY* ············

When a new dog owner begins raising a puppy and finishes their basic training, many come to the conclusion that they are DONE maintaining their puppy's basic needs.

They often think, "Well I'm glad that's over, now all I have to do is feed and exercise my pup, and I have no worries!"

* * * *Facepalm* * * *

Don't be this person! **I can't stress enough how crucial it is to your puppy's long-term health and happiness to keep them well groomed.**

Why?

Hang on tight; I'm about to explain soon.

.... Those who instill FEAR into their puppy when grooming due to a lack of knowledge and grooming protocol: ....

Equally as harmful can be the dog owners who care deeply about their puppy and their grooming needs. However, they misunderstand how to go about this process and have most likely skipped crucial steps along the way.

Of course, you want your pup to be well behaved when he's at the groomer or the vet. However, **it's imperative that your pup is accustomed to allowing people to touch him BEFORE putting him in new environments.**

Here's how to create comfort for your puppy in preparation for grooming and veterinary activities:

🐾 **From the time you bring your pup home, you should touch your puppy on all his body parts so that he is used to it and doesn't get scared or aggressive when he is at the groomer or vet.**

- Touch all of his limbs and tail.

- Touch everything on your puppy's head—his ears, nose, open his mouth, etc.

- A lot of dogs are sensitive on their feet, so be sure to touch his feet often and in between his paws as well.

  ★ When dogs are not used to people touching certain parts of them, they get very nervous and could attempt to bite the person out of fear.

- **This will get your pup used to being touched all around and will make him much more friendly and trusting of the people that are trying to help him.**

BRIGHT IDEAS

Upon bringing your puppy home, get him prepared for grooming activities by touching him all around. When paired with proper socialization with other people, this will get him used to hands touching him and make him much more comfortable with being groomed by strangers.

Q *What are my puppy's grooming needs?*

Here is a question I often receive from new puppy owners who are highly motivated to account for all of their pup's needs. However, the answer is one that varies depending on the dog (how convenient, I know). **Grooming needs vary between all breeds, and a puppy's grooming needs may change when he is an adult.** With that in mind, here is a list of the basic grooming needs that should be maintained for all puppies:

- Nail Trimming
- Bathing
- Brushing Teeth
- Brushing Fur
- Ear Cleaning

❧ NAIL TRIMMING

Long, unkempt nails not only look unattractive but over time they can do irreparable damage to your puppy. When dog nails are so long that they consistently touch the ground, they exert force back into the nail bed with every step, creating pain for your pup and pressure on the toe joint. To humanize this kind of pain, think of wearing a shoe that is too small for your foot, and having this immensely uncomfortable force pushing against your long, uncut nails back into your inflamed nail bed. Doesn't sound too fun, does it?

Long term, this state can compromise your dog's weight distribution and natural alignment, which can leave him more susceptible to injuries, and make walking and running difficult and painful. Ultimately, unattended nails create a vicious cycle. Since long nails make any contact with your puppy's paws painful for him, he will begin to avoid having them touched, which leads to unpleasant nail-trimming sessions, which makes both human and dog avoid them, which leads to longer intervals between trims, which leads to more pain.

> **Q** *How often should I trim my puppy's nails? What's the "correct" length of a dog's nails?*

While some dogs are often groomed with nails so incredibly short they can barely be seen, **the most commonly accepted rule of thumb is that when a dog is standing, the nails should not make contact with the ground.** Therefore, if you can hear your pup's nails making contact with the floor as he comes towards you, then his nails are too long. Based on the destructive consequences for your pup and the pain that arises from uncut nails, you should trim your puppy's nails about once a week. Therefore, start trimming your puppy's nails right away so that it doesn't end up being a dreadful event for either of you.

BRIGHT IDEAS

Keep your puppy's nails well kept by clipping them once a week to avoid a vicious cycle of pain for your pup.

Q *How do I cut my puppy's nails?*

While many people are apprehensive about trimming their pup's nails, **it's really not as hard as you think!** As you know by now, it indeed is crucial to maintain a consistent nail clipping routine, but it doesn't need to be an ordeal that gives you anxiety every time you think about it!

What can make trimming nails tricky and potentially dangerous for new dog owners is the anatomy of a dog's nails—don't worry, I'm not going to bring you back to high school anatomy class! Dog nails have a nerve and vein running through them called the "quick." Avoid cutting near it. Why, you may ask? Cutting this sensitive band of tissue is very painful for the dog—and messy for you, as blood often drains from the cut nail for what seems like an eternity.

KEYS TO SUCCESS

When clipping your puppy's nails, avoid cutting near the "quick," a sensitive nerve and vein that runs through your pup's nail.

Q *So what is the proper way to clip my puppy's nails?*

Your pup will either have <u>white nails</u> or <u>dark nails</u>. White nails are definitely easier to trim, but dark nails are not as difficult as many people seem to think they are.

Here is a simple guide to follow when cutting your puppy's nails:

················ *Puppies with <u>white</u> nails* ················

🐕 **Begin by identifying the quick.**

- In puppies with white nails, you can identify the quick as the pink-colored area within your puppy's nail.

🐕 If you are using a clipper or scissors, trim a bit off the end of the nail, and notice the color at the end of the nail when looking at it directly.

🐕 **As soon as the center of the nail starts to appear pink, stop.**

🐕 Do not cut too far into the nail or you will hit the quick.

················ *Puppies with <u>dark</u> nails* ················

🐕 **Begin by identifying the quick.**

- In puppies with dark nails, it's difficult to determine the quick with the naked eye.

  ★ Therefore, with darker nails, you have to be even more conservative about how much you trim off.

- After making each cut, look at the nail.

- **If you see a black spot in the center, then stop clipping.**

  ★ It's likely your next cut will puncture the quick.

- Do not cut too far into the nail or you will hit the quick.

Q *What happens if I cut my dog's nail too far?*

If you cut into the quick, it will bleed a lot. Honestly, for a new dog owner it will seem like quite a lot of blood coming from just a small nail, so **don't be overly worried if it seems like the nail is bleeding profusely.** The best way to stop the bleeding is by using a styptic powder like "Kwik Stop" to promote blood clotting. If you don't have a styptic powder such as this on hand, put baking soda on the bleeding nail and apply pressure. It will probably take a few minutes to stop the bleeding, so keep applying pressure.

Please refer to the drawing below on how to properly restrain your pup while trimming his nails.

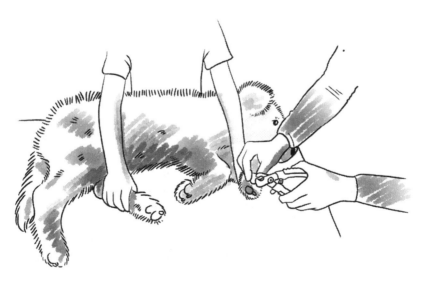

THE CORRECT WAY TO TRIM YOUR PUP'S NAILS

❧ BATHING

Some clients have told me that they have heard it is not good to bathe a puppy until he is six months old. This couldn't be further from the truth! **No matter what age your puppy is, he's never too young to be bathed.**

Q *What are the benefits of bathing my puppy young?*

🐾 Getting them acclimated to and comfortable with being bathed.

- You need to introduce baths to a puppy early on so that he won't fear them!

- Trust me, giving a bath to a dog that fears or despises bath time is NOT fun.

  * To prevent this, give your pup treats while he's in the bath and give him physical affection.

  ★ **This associates baths with positivity.**

🐾 **Getting your pup used to taking a bath at a young age will prevent stress and issues in the future.**

- Regardless of whether you have a high-energy or reserved puppy, waiting six months (or a long stretch of time) to introduce him to bathing will make the acclimation process much more stressful for both you and your pup!

  ★ As described earlier, it's much easier to mold a puppy when he is several weeks old as opposed to several months old, not only because puppies are more malleable at a younger age but also because they're easier to handle in terms of size.

> ### Bright Ideas
>
> Beginning to bathe your puppy at a young age will get him comfortable with being bathed and help prevent bathing issues in the future.

Q *How often should I bathe my puppy?*

There's a lot of controversy as to what the correct answer to this question is. As a general rule of thumb, most experts such as myself suggest that you should plan to bathe your pup **once a month**. A dog really doesn't need a bath until you think he does, meaning when he smells or appears to be dirty. However, planning for a bath once a month may mean that you end up bathing your pup more than that. On the other hand, you also need to be aware that you shouldn't bathe your puppy more than twice a month (if possible). Bathing a dog too often can be harmful because his fur and skin will be stripped of the essential natural oils needed to stay healthy.

Q *Are there any exceptions to the once a month rule?*

Remember what this book was designed to be: a guide, and not a rulebook! Raising a puppy is supposed to be a fun and incredibly fulfilling journey, not an overly compulsive drill. As a passionate dog owner myself, I wholeheartedly understand that you want to do everything in your power to give your pup the best life possible. However, keep in mind that things don't always work out as planned and you need to be flexible sometimes!

Therefore, you might end up giving your pup his once-a-month bath, and then the next week your pup ends up rolling in a puddle of mud. Yes, you will need to give your puppy another bath, and that is alright!

You just don't want to get into the habit of giving your pup a bath too often, such as once a week.

Q *Does the type of shampoo matter?*

Yes, it certainly does. **Your pup needs puppy shampoo.** He is a baby, so his skin is still very sensitive. Adult shampoos sometimes contain chemicals or odors that are too strong for puppies, so **the general rule of thumb is to use puppy shampoo until your pup is at least one year old.** In addition, investing in high-quality shampoos throughout your dog's life is very beneficial. High-quality shampoos are a lot gentler on your pup's skin and fur, whereas low-quality (usually the cheapest) shampoos often contain ingredients that can irritate your pup's skin. If your pup has extremely sensitive skin and seems uncomfortable after using even a high-quality shampoo, try a hypoallergenic one.

Q *Does my puppy need conditioner?*

Conditioner is not a necessity for any dog, but it can be very beneficial. **Conditioners help to hydrate and moisturize your pup's coat. If your pup has longer hair, conditioner is very helpful with detangling as well.**

KEYS TO SUCCESS

Plan to bathe your pup once a month. Keep in mind that if you bathe your puppy more often than this on a consistent basis, his fur and skin will be stripped of the essential natural oils needed to stay healthy.

🐾 BRUSHING TEETH

Q *Do I really need to brush my puppy's teeth?*

Absolutely! Brushing your puppy's teeth is extremely important for proper dental hygiene. To ensure that you do this properly, here is a list of tips to assist you through this process:

- Start brushing your pup's teeth when you're getting him acclimated into your home and get into a consistent routine of doing it.

- Starting when your puppy is young is imperative so that he will grow to be used to it his whole life.

- Yes, he will lose all of his baby teeth between four and six months old, but it's still important to keep him healthy and get him comfortable with you putting your hands in his mouth.

- Dogs who have never had their teeth brushed are very skeptical when you try to do it which makes it much more difficult.

Q *How often do I need to brush my puppy's teeth?*

I aim to brush my dog's teeth once or twice a week. Just like in humans, the food your pup eats can get stuck in his teeth and will cause plaque build up. It's not going to hurt your pup if you miss a week of teeth brushing, but try your best to do it regularly. It really doesn't take that long!

❧ BRUSHING FUR

Remember, every breed of dog has different grooming needs. Hair brushing ultimately depends on your pup's breed and his unique coat. If your dog has extremely short hair, like a Boxer or Great Dane, it probably won't be necessary to brush your pup nearly as much as a long haired dog such as an Australian Shepherd, which you should brush daily. Even if your pup has medium length fur, you should make sure to brush him regularly to keep the fur from matting. There are a variety of different types of brushes that cater to the variety of different needs for hair brushing. Do some research on your dog's particular breed to find out which brush type will work best for your pup.

Although it may not be necessary to brush your puppy's fur (depending on his breed) it will be very beneficial no matter how long their coat is. **Brushing a pup's coat is helpful in balancing and evening out the natural oils in the fur, and promotes healthy skin growth.** As with other grooming chores, brushing is also beneficial in that it allows your pup to get accustomed to someone touching him all over.

When brushing your pup, constantly praise him for sitting still and allowing you to brush him. Make fur brushing a fun time!

KEYS TO SUCCESS

Brushing your puppy is beneficial for balancing out the natural oils in the fur, promoting healthy skin growth, and getting him used to someone touching him all over.

🐾 Ear Cleaning

Although you may be surprised to find out, **cleaning your puppy's ears is very important for his hygiene and health.** Dirt and bacteria often get into dogs' ears and must be cleaned out. If your pup's ears aren't cleaned, it can lead to him having ear infections.

Q *How often should I clean my puppy's ears?*

You should clean your puppy's ears once a week. You can get ear-cleaning solution from any pet store. Here's a simple method to clean your pup's ears:

- Pour some of the ear cleaning solution into your puppy's ears.

- Gently massage the ears from the outside for about 30 seconds.

- Let your puppy shake out his ears.

- Use a cotton ball to clean all over the ear to remove the remaining dirt and bacteria.

- Only clean as far as your finger will fit in the ear.

- Never try to stick a Q-tip or other cleaning item down into your dog's ear—it can really damage the ear canal.

If you notice that your puppy's ears are red, inflamed, and/or have a foul smelling odor coming from them, **do not** attempt to clean them yourself and schedule a vet appointment for your pup ASAP.

Veterinary Knowledge 101

.... 🐾 ....

I'd like to pre-empt this section by noting that I'm not a veterinarian and I'm not qualified in terms of a certification to give professional advice. The following information are my opinions and ideas based on my own 10+ years of experience in the dog industry. With that in mind, I feel extremely confident providing you with knowledge derived from my own experience studying Animal Science in college and working in the emergency care unit of a veterinary specialty hospital.

Q *How do I know if something is wrong with my puppy?*

It is very common for first-time puppy owners to get nervous when anything is off about their puppy, no matter how small. Whether you're unsure why your puppy is being lethargic when he's typically full of energy, or you're worried about him not eating enough, there are a number of reasons that could cause a new puppy owner to become concerned.

Being concerned about the livelihood of your puppy is understandable; however, never try to make judgments on your puppy's health that should be entrusted to a vet. And no, relying on the internet is not 'just as good.' If you have never had a dog before, you really don't know what is normal and what is not. If you are ever unsure, give your veterinarian a call or bring your puppy in to get checked out. It is better to be safe than sorry.

Now, having said that, **this section can save you thousands of dollars if you take it to heart.** While I may not be a veterinarian by title or certification, I DO have loads of invaluable experience that can save you hundreds to thousands of dollars in unnecessary vet bills. I have worked "in the trenches," so to speak, of vet hospitals, where I have witnessed naive dog owners (which, to their defense, just care deeply about their puppy and don't know any better), bring their pup to the vet for a mild or minor case that ends up costing them upwards of $1000 or more.

In writing this book, it has been one of my principal goals to help new dog owners such as you SAVE this kind of time and money that you may have lost if not for learning the principles in this handbook. With that in mind, **the largest costs you will incur over your dog's lifetime will be shockingly expensive vet bills.** Veterinary bills can be VERY expensive and sometimes unnecessary.

BRIGHT IDEAS

Following the suggestions in this section and applying its key principles can save you HUNDREDS of dollars over your puppy's life span.

After reading through the rest of this section, you will have a better understanding regarding these areas of basic puppy veterinary care:

🐾 Gum Color and CRT

🐾 Temperature

🐾 Bowel Movements

🐾 Supplements To Give Your Puppy

🐾 Basic Wound Care

🐾 How To Give Your Puppy Pills

🐾 Socialization

🐾 Common Illnesses In Puppies

- Parvovirus

- Kennel Cough

- Distemper

🐾 Fleas And Ticks

🐾 Vaccinations

🐾 Heartworm Pills

🐾 Getting Your Puppy Fixed

🐾 GUM COLOR AND CRT

Gum color is one of the best indicators of a dog's health. When checking your puppy's gums, <u>pink gum color is an indication of good health</u>.

Q *Do I want my puppy's gums to be light or dark pink?*

Gum color will get lighter and lighter the less healthy your puppy is. The degree of pinkness varies within dogs, so be sure to check your pup's normal gum color. This is important because some dogs have lighter pink gums to begin with, which is completely fine, but you need to know your pup's normal gum color as a foundation for future comparison.

BRIGHT IDEAS

Gum color is one of the most accurate indicators of a dog's health. Know your puppy's healthy gum color and monitor it if you sense that your puppy isn't feeling well.

Q *When should I be concerned?*

Whenever one of my dogs is acting a little bit abnormal, I immediately will check his gum color. If your pup's gum color is a little lighter than usual, be sure to keep a close eye on your pup and his health. It's usually not a major issue if the gums are a little lighter. If, however, your puppy's gums are extremely light (pale) this is a cause for concern. Pale gums can be a result of a number of different issues, and I suggest bringing your pup to the vet ASAP.

Other causes for concern with gum color would be if the gums were yellow, blue, or a darker color such as gray or black. While I'm not a registered veterinarian (yet), here is what I can tell you about different colored gums from my experience of working on the floor of an emergency care veterinarian hospital:

🐕 Yellow Gums

- **If a dog's gums have a yellow tint**—for all you veterinary nerds out there, this condition is called icteric—**this indicates a serious issue with the dog's red blood cells and requires immediate veterinary attention.**

🐕 Blue Gums

- **This indicates a lack of oxygen and would require immediate veterinary attention.**

🐕 Dark Gum Color (Gray or Black)

- **Darker gum color is a serious issue and could mean your dog is in serious shock.**

  ★ Some dogs' gums have a black pigment to begin with, which gives no indication of bad health, so make sure you know what your dog's gum color looks like normally.

Again, if your pup is experiencing any abnormalities in gum color, you should bring him to the vet *immediately.*

🐾 How To Check CRT

If you are still concerned about your puppy's health, along with checking your dog's gum color, you can check the capillary refill time (CRT) of your dog's gums. To check your puppy's CRT:

- Press on your dog's gums with your finger gently.

- In the spot where you press your finger, the gum will turn pale.

- Remove your finger and count how long it takes for the gum to return to its normal color.

  - This is the capillary refill time, which should be no more than one to two seconds. **If the CRT is longer than two seconds, you should consult your veterinarian right away.**

❧ TEMPERATURE

If you suspect that your pup might be feeling under the weather, you can take his temperature. You can purchase a dog thermometer or use a human digital thermometer.

Q *How do I take my puppy's temperature?*

Unlike with a person, you will not insert the thermometer under your puppy's tongue to take his temperature. Rectal temperatures will give you the most accurate reading of your puppy's temperature. **A dog's normal temperature is 99.0° to 102.5°F.** You will also definitely want to restrain your dog properly while taking his temperatures. If you don't, he may get scared when he feels something going into his rectum and snap back at you. Or, your puppy may just sit down, and you won't be able to get the thermometer into him.

··········· *How to properly take your pup's temperature* ···········

🐾 You will likely need **two** people—one to restrain and one to put the thermometer into his rectum.

🐾 Make sure your dog is standing up and sit by his side.

🐾 Wrap one arm around his neck to keep his head from going back.

🐾 Put the other arm under his stomach and around up to his back.

🐾 Once you have a firm grip, the other person should slowly insert the thermometer.

🐾 Wait a few seconds and remove thermometer to get your reading.

Some dogs really despise having their temperature taken. However, your pup will get more accustomed to it the more he gets his temperature taken, and as always, it's easier to accustom your pup to uncomfortable situations while he's young. Make sure you are praising your puppy and giving him treats while taking his temperature.

BRIGHT IDEAS

Have another person help you restrain your pup if you ever need to take his temperature.

❧ BOWEL MOVEMENTS

Your pup's bowel movements are also a great indicator of his health. For this reason, you should always keep notice of your dog's stool.

Your puppy's stool should be solid for the most part. Things to be worried about in your pup's bowel movements are:

- **Diarrhea**
- **Blood In Stool**
- **Mucus In Stool**
- **Constipation**

Diarrhea, the most common of the above, is the term given to any stool that is loose or liquid in nature. **Diarrhea is a symptom of something gone wrong in the dog's gastrointestinal tract.**

KEYS TO SUCCESS

Always keep notice of your dog's stool. Your pup's bowel movements are another great indicator of your dog's health.

Q *Why would my puppy have diarrhea?*

There are two types of diarrhea: acute and chronic. Acute diarrhea is fairly common in puppies. Puppies will get into things and eat stuff that they are not supposed to—this is practically inevitable. Often when a puppy eats something outside of his normal diet, it will upset his stomach and likely cause diarrhea. This is the most common cause of diarrhea in puppies, but there are many other causes as well.

Change in a puppy's life or certain medications can most certainly cause diarrhea as I explained earlier in this book.

Diarrhea can also be a symptom of more serious illnesses in puppies, such as parvovirus, in which diarrhea would be chronic. **It's vital to keep track of every bowel movement if your puppy has abnormalities in his stool.** If your pup is having diarrhea for more than two weeks or is having it constantly, this would be chronic diarrhea. If your pup is having chronic diarrhea, I suggest making an appointment with your veterinarian.

❧ SUPPLEMENTS

Q *What supplements should I be giving my puppy?*

This is a very common question I get from a lot of puppy owners, especially given the newly popular dog vitamin market. The answer is simple: **If you are feeding your puppy a high-quality puppy food, you do not need to be giving your puppy any additional supplements.** Yes, that's correct—your puppy doesn't need ANY supplements. High-quality foods are created with all of the vitamins and minerals your puppy needs!

Not only are additional supplements not necessary, they can actually be harmful to your pup. If you are giving your puppy an excess of certain vitamins or minerals, it can be toxic. Don't fall prey to the claims of dog supplement companies that lack any scientific foundations. If you aren't sure that your puppy's food is sufficient in providing your pup with all the essential vitamins and minerals he needs, consult your veterinarian.

🐾 Basic Wound Care

A lot of first-time dog owners get very concerned with every scrape and scratch their puppy gets, which is entirely understandable. If you have never owned a dog before, it's often difficult to differentiate a wound that needs veterinary attention from one that doesn't. **If you are unsure, it's always in your puppy's best interest to bring him to the vet.** What I tell my clients is if the wound's surface area is large or is deeper than just the top layer of skin, you should bring your puppy to the veterinarian.

However, if your pup has a minor wound that doesn't quite need veterinary attention, here's what you should do to help speed up the healing process:

🐾 Wash the wound with an antiseptic solution composed of CHLORHEXIDINE diluted with water.

🐾 If the wound is in a location that can be bandaged, cut a telfa (non-adhesive) pad the size of the wound and place on top of the wound.

🐾 Use a compression bandage wrap to hold telfa pad in place and wrap around the outside of the bandage area to keep it in place.

🐾 Use a piece of waterproof tape to tape the end of the bandage.

❧ How To Give Your Dog Pills

A lot of first-time dog owners are nervous or unsure of how to properly give their dogs medication. However, I can almost guarantee that you will have to give your pup a pill at some point in his life, so this is an important skill to know how to execute properly.

First, **try wrapping the pill in food that your puppy will LOVE (such as cheese or peanut butter).** Hopefully, your pup will devour the treat. Unfortunately, sometimes our dogs are smarter than we think and know that there's a pill wrapped inside. Juneau loves to maneuver the pill out of the treat in her mouth, swallow the treat, and then spit out the pill. Such a stinker! I find that it's a lot more common for adult dogs to catch on to your tricky 'pilling' method than for puppies. However, there are puppies that will spit out the pill too. If this happens, you are going to have to "pill" your pup. To do this:

- 🐾 Open up your puppy's mouth.

- 🐾 Put the pill as far back into his throat as you can.

- 🐾 Gently close his mouth and hold your hand around it.

- 🐾 Blow on his nose or gently rub his throat with your other hand until he swallows the pill.

- 🐾 If your puppy is very stubborn, it may take a while before he actually swallows the pill, so be patient.

🐾 COMMON ILLNESSES IN PUPPIES

🐕 Parvovirus

- **Parvo is a HORRIBLE virus and can be fatal. It weakens a puppy's immune system and slowly kills him.**

- More commonly known as Parvo, this is a highly contagious virus among dogs.

  - ★ Puppies are most susceptible to Parvo because they aren't yet fully vaccinated and have weaker immune systems.

- Parvo is spread through contact with an infected dog or through contact with an infected dog's feces.

- Symptoms of Parvo:

  - ★ Excessive and chronic diarrhea

  - ★ Excessive and chronic vomiting

  - ★ Lethargy

  - ★ Anorexia

  - ★ Fever

- **If you believe that your puppy may have parvovirus, take him to the emergency veterinarian IMMEDIATELY.**

🐕 Kennel Cough

- **Kennel cough is a virus distinguished by a coughing or hacking sound.**

★ If your pup consistently is hacking like he has something stuck in his throat or is always coughing, he may have kennel cough.

• Kennel cough is much like the human cold. It can be caused by a number of different viruses. Dogs catch kennel cough by breathing in the virus, and then an infection of the respiratory tract begins.

• **Kennel cough is commonly spread in highly populated and crowded areas of dogs.**

• Kennel cough sounds horrible but often does not need veterinary treatment.

  ★ Since it's caused by a virus, it must run its course.

  ★ The coughing and hacking will slowly subside.

• You should see improvements within one week and the symptoms completely gone within three weeks.

.... ❤ ....

🐾 Distemper

• **Distemper is a horrible infectious disease that affects the nervous system and can be fatal.**

• Puppies are first vaccinated against distemper usually between 6-8 weeks. This vaccination is highly effective, but as with all vaccinations, there is a chance that the puppy can still contract the virus.

• **Symptoms of Distemper:**

  ★ Fever

  ★ Discharge from nose and eyes

★ Lethargy

★ Difficulty breathing and/or coughing

★ Seizures

- **If you believe that your puppy may have Distemper, bring him to the vet IMMEDIATELY.**

❧ FLEAS AND TICKS

Fleas and ticks can cause more serious problems in young puppies than in adult dogs, but regardless of your dog's age, they are pesky insects you want off of your pup ASAP.

Fleas

Dogs often become infested with fleas during the summer months as fleas thrive in warmer weather.

Q *How does my puppy get infested with fleas?*

Dogs will get fleas from other animals or just from the environment. Fleas have the ability to jump from host to host, biting as they go. Fleabites will cause dogs' skin to itch and result in your dog scratching constantly. Sometimes, however, a dog's skin will itch for reasons other than fleabites so be sure that fleas are the culprits before proceeding with treatment.

If your pup has fleas, you should be able to see them in his fur. They like to go in hidden areas like behind the ears, around the neck, and around your dog's rear as well. They usually hang out close to the skin, so you may have to separate your dog's hair and look closely. If you see specks about the size of a small grain of rice scurrying around in your pet's fur, he's got fleas.

If you don't see fleas directly, you may see their feces, which is also an indicator that your dog is infested. Flea feces will look like little black pepper flakes. To be sure it indeed is flea feces, put one of the flakes on a paper towel and then put a little water on it. You should see it turn to a reddish-brown color, the color of blood since flea feces are made up of digested blood.

Q *What should I do if my puppy has fleas?*

Now that you know your dog certainly has fleas, you can follow these next steps. **If you don't know for certain, it may be wise to schedule a vet appointment so he or she can tell you for sure.** Also, if your dog has itchy skin due to something other than fleas, you may want your vet to take a look at your pup. Note: you must consult your veterinarian before administering a flea treatment to your puppy, as some of them aren't safe for puppies under a certain age. Also, talk to your vet about when is a proper time to start a flea preventative treatment on your puppy.

The problem with fleas is that once they have infested your dog, they are in your house as well. **You are going to have to kill them off in your house and on your dog.** If you only treat your dog, the fleas in your house will just jump right back onto him, and the cycle will start again.

How to get rid of fleas in your home:

- Vacuum, vacuum, vacuum! Fleas love to live in your carpets so make sure to vacuum everywhere multiple times.

- Sweep, mop, and deep clean your entire house.

- Use an anti-flea treatment across your house with a product that your veterinarian recommends. Your vet will most likely tell you to repeat this process after a week or two.

- Throw out your pup's bedding

  - This is the easiest way to get rid of the fleas on your dog's blankets or beds.

  - **If you don't want to throw it out, you can buy an anti-flea detergent and wash it multiple times.**

Q How should I treat my flea-infested pup?

Be sure to ask your veterinarian what he or she recommends for treating your pup for fleas, but I will share with you what has worked in my experiences with flea-infested dogs:

🐾 **Use a fast-acting flea removal product from your veterinarian (Capstar works wonders).**

- This will require you to bring your pup to the vet.

🐾 **If you cannot get to the veterinarian immediately or you just want to provide immediate relief to your pup, you can use a flea comb on your pup.**

- Fill a bucket with hot water and dish soap.

- Comb through your pup's fur with the flea comb.

  ★ You should be able to see fleas on the teeth of the comb.

- Put the fleas in the bucket of soapy water to kill them.

- Repeat this all over your puppy's body.

- This will help relieve your puppy of some of the itchiness he has been enduring and get rid of some of the fleas.

🐾 **Give your puppy a bath with a veterinarian-recommended puppy anti-flea shampoo.**

- **Make sure it is safe to use on puppies!**

- Also, make sure you fill the bathtub high so that your pup is submerged in the water.

  ★ Drowning the fleas is one way to kill some of them.

- Lather on the anti-flea shampoo generously all over your puppy's body.

🐾 **Give your pup the medication your veterinarian has provided to you to kill off the remaining fleas.**

·············· *Ticks* ··············

Ugh, ticks are so disgusting and honestly creep me out. **I hate ticks.** They find a host, cling on and feed off of the host's blood. Often ticks also carry diseases that are transmitted to the host. Unfortunately, dogs make excellent hosts for ticks. Once a tick attaches onto a host, it can spread a disease in 24-48 hours, so it is important that you find and remove any ticks on your dog **immediately**.

Anytime your dog goes outside, he faces the risk of a tick attaching to him, even if you have given him a tick prevention treatment. Ask your veterinarian for recommendations of tick prevention medication. It's important to check your puppy's body all over after he has been outside. **Check EVERYWHERE.** Ticks love to hide out in hidden places like behind the ears and in between the toes. If you feel a bump, check to see if it is a tick because it could have burrowed under your pup's skin already. If this happens, please contact your veterinarian.

Q *What kind of diseases can a tick transmit to my puppy?*

Common tick-borne diseases include:

🐾 **Lyme Disease**

- The most common tick-borne disease

  ★ Comes from deer ticks

- **Symptoms usually don't start to occur until 2-5 months after the deer tick bite.**

- The most common symptoms are as follows:

  - ★ Fever

  - ★ Lameness

  - ★ Swollen limbs

  - ★ Loss of appetite

  - ★ Lethargy

  - ★ Depression

  - ★ Weight loss

- **If you suspect that your dog may have Lyme disease, bring him to the vet IMMEDIATELY.**

  - ★ With proper and immediate veterinary care, Lyme disease is treatable. **If left untreated, Lyme disease is fatal.**

🐾 Rocky Mountain Spotted Fever

- Comes from the wood tick, the lone star tick, and the American dog tick.

- **Symptoms appear suddenly and include:**

  - ★ Stiffness

  - ★ Neurological problems

  - ★ Skin lesions

- **If you think your dog may have been infected with this disease, bring him to a veterinarian IMMEDIATELY.**

★ If left untreated, Rocky Mountain Spotted Fever **can be fatal.**

Q *How do I remove a tick off of my puppy?*

🐕 **Put on gloves.**

- Ticks have the ability to transmit diseases to humans too, so make sure you wear gloves.

🐕 **Have another person restrain your pup and keep him calm.**

🐕 **Use tweezers to grip onto the tick's body and pull it straight out.**

- It's important to pull straight out instead of trying to twist it loose so that you end up pulling the entire tick out.

- Otherwise, the head may stay attached, which makes it harder to remove.

🐕 Often a veterinarian will recommend that you put the tick into a container of isopropyl alcohol.

- This will kill the tick and also preserve it for tests later on if you suspect your dog may have been infected with a tick-borne disease.

❧ VACCINATIONS

Vaccines help protect your puppy against potentially fatal diseases and other health issues. **As an avid dog lover, pre-veterinary student, and former veterinary assistant, I can tell you with 100% honesty and genuine care that it's absolutely imperative that you follow your veterinarian's instructions on when to get each puppy shot and booster so that your puppy is fully protected.** Young puppies receive immunity from viruses and diseases from their mother's milk, but after they are weaned off of their mother, this immunity fades.

Q *Is it possible to over-vaccinate my puppy?*

Similar to the vaccination controversy surrounding children, there is some controversy in vaccinating dogs. However, keep this in mind: the discussion is not centered on whether puppies should be vaccinated, as most people agree that vaccinations are necessary to ensure immunity. Rather, where the controversy lies is AFTER your pup is done with his puppy vaccines. Many people disagree on how often your dog needs to receive "suggested" vaccinations.

Don't get me wrong, over-vaccination does happen. However, instead of not vaccinating your puppy at all, PLEASE do your homework on what vaccinations are "suggested" as opposed to those that are crucial to your puppy's long-term health. Again, it's VERY important that you educate yourself on vaccinations. Different states may vary in their vaccine laws or guidelines a little bit, so make sure to consult your veterinary office to find out what they recommend for your state.

KEYS TO SUCCESS

Make sure you get your puppy the necessary vaccinations that he needs to live a long, healthy life. When it comes to additional vaccinations, consult your veterinarian and do your own research so that you can make an educated decision.

Q *How can I keep track of all my puppy's vaccinations?*

It's crucial to find out which vaccinations, if any, your puppy already received prior to you bringing him home. **To keep this information organized, I created a folder for each of my dog's vet records.** Do this from the start to make things easier as your pup ages and matures! Also, it's very smart to create a document to keep track of the vaccines and medications your pup has received and the dates that he received them, whether in print or on your computer. It's important to keep all documentation of your puppy's vaccinations, so either try the solution I've offered here or play around with other options to find the best fit for your personal organization needs.

Q *What vaccinations does my puppy need?*

A lot of people get very confused when it comes to what vaccinations their puppy needs. I will give you the basic guidelines on what each vaccine is and when your puppy needs them so that you can get a better understanding of why you need each vaccination, as opposed to just blindly following recommendations. **Remember that these are only basic guidelines that can vary slightly depending on your location and you should always follow your vet's recommendations.**

The Three Main Puppy Vaccines:

🐕 DHPP

- **DHPP stands for Distemper, Hepatitis, Parvovirus, and Parainfluenza—the viruses it protects against.**

- **DHPP is the most common vaccine given to dogs.**

- It is ideal to vaccinate your puppy as early as possible. This vaccine can be given to puppies starting at **six weeks** of age.

  - ★ If started at **six weeks**, a series of **four vaccines** will need to be given, each at **three weeks apart.**

  - ★ If started later at nine weeks, a series of three vaccines will need to be given, each at three weeks apart.

  - ★ If started at 12 weeks or later, a series of two vaccines will need to be given, each at three weeks apart.

.... 🐾 ....

🐕 Bordetella

- **This vaccine protects puppies against Kennel Cough.**

- Bordetella is given to your puppy no earlier than at eleven weeks of age.

- Most dog daycares or kennels will not allow your puppy at their facility until your pup has had this vaccine.

- Depending on your veterinarian, your puppy will receive Bordetella in injectable or nasal form.

  - ★ The injectable form is given in a series of **two**, each at **three weeks apart.**

  - ★ The nasal form is given every **six months**.

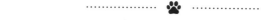

🐕 Rabies

- As many of you probably already know, Rabies is an extremely serious disease.

  ★ **If a dog contracts rabies, it's** *always fatal.*

- Thus, protection against this terrible disease is 100% necessary.

- **Rabies vaccinations for dogs are required by law in the majority of U.S. states.**

- Depending on the laws in your state, the Rabies vaccine is given once between the ages of 12-16 weeks old.

❦ HEARTWORM MEDICATION

Heartworms are transmitted to dogs through mosquitoes. Every time a mosquito bites your dog, he has the potential to be exposed to heartworms.

Q *How do I prevent my dogs from getting heartworms?*

Heartworm is very difficult to treat, but very easy to prevent. You should begin treating your pup for heartworm right away at around eight weeks old. Almost all heartworm medication is safe for puppies at that age, but be sure to double check with your veterinarian to see what he or she recommends.

Q *How often should I give my pup heartworm medication?*

Once you've begun to treat your pup for heartworms, **it's crucial to give your puppy the correct dose of heartworm medication every 30 days.** Although most call it prevention, the medication actually kills heartworms if your dog has contracted them. It is extremely effective in killing baby heartworm.

If a dog is bitten by a mosquito and is infected with heartworms, these heartworms will be babies for 45-60 days. After that, the heartworms will be older and much harder to treat. **This is why it's so important to never skip a dose!** If you give your dog his heartworm medication on June 1 and he gets bitten by a mosquito on June 2, he can still get infected with heartworms. They will remain babies for 45-60 days, so you must give him his dose on the correct date of July 1 to kill these baby heartworms.

Q *I live in a state where there are no mosquitoes during the winter. Do I still need to give my dog heartworm medication during these months?*

Yes. To ensure your pup's health year-round it's smart to keep him on heartworm medication throughout every season. Consult your veterinarian with any more questions about heartworm or to determine which heartworm prevention medication is best for your pup.

❀ GETTING YOUR DOG FIXED

You 100% absolutely, definitely, positively MUST get your puppy spayed or neutered!

Q *Why do I need to get my puppy fixed?*

The United States, as well as many other countries around the world, has millions of homeless dogs that end up at shelters and then get euthanized every single year. **That's right, millions of healthy, happy, friendly dogs are killed in the United States every year.** We as a society *must* reduce this number drastically. The only way to do this is to spay and neuter your dogs to stop increasing the number of dogs being born.

It's also why I am such a huge advocate of adopting a pet instead of buying a pet from a breeder. There are millions of dogs already in need of homes at shelters and rescues, and if they do not get adopted they face the chance of being euthanized. While this is going on, millions of puppies are being born as the result of breeding. How does it make any sense that millions of healthy dogs are being euthanized because there is not enough room for them, but breeders are bringing millions more puppies into the world?

KEYS TO SUCCESS

Getting your puppy fixed is ABSOLUTELY necessary. Not only does it limit behavioral and sexual complications in the future, but it also will help your dog live a longer and healthier life.

If my rant above did not convince you to spay or neuter your puppy, then how about the fact that fixing your pup will improve his health and lengthen his lifespan? Yep, your dog will live a longer and healthier life if you get him fixed. For females especially, spaying your pup helps prevent the risk of her developing uterine infections or tumors in the ovaries, uterus, and breasts. For males, neutering your puppy will reduce the risk of testicular cancer and prostate issues.

More reasons why you should spay your female puppy:

🐾 She will not go into heat

- Do you really want to have to deal with your dog having her period all over the house? I didn't think so.

🐾 She will not get pregnant

- Of course, this is the main reason why you want to spay your female, but right now I'm talking about the actual process of your pup having to undergo pregnancy and having puppies, which can lead to complications.

More reasons why you should neuter your male puppy:

🐾 He will be less likely to try to escape and roam

- An unneutered male feels the need to go out and find a mate, and that will cause him to attempt to escape and roam.

    ★ Neutering your male reduces this need greatly.

🐾 He will be calmer

- Neutering reduces the testosterone levels in your puppy and will result in him acting a lot calmer towards people and other dogs.

🐾 He will be less aggressive

- If your male pup is being too aggressive with other dogs, neutering him will significantly reduce this.

    ★ **Unneutered males feel the need to assert dominance on other male dogs,** while it is a lot less common for neutered males to feel this need.

🐾 **It will reduce his sexual behaviors**

- If your dog constantly tries to mount other dogs, neutering him will drastically mitigate this temptation.

    ★ With lower testosterone levels, your male pup will not feel the need to hump other dogs as much or as often.

Note: I'm not saying that neutering your dog will COMPLETELY fix these behaviors, but it WILL reduce them.

Living Life With The Dog Of Your Dreams

Congrats! You've made it through the entire handbook! Since you've put in the time and made it all the way to the end of this extensive guide, you should feel <u>very</u> proud for putting yourself in the best possible position to raise a well-behaved AND well-trained pup!

Using the tools, techniques, and hopefully, the *skills* you've gained from reading and practicing the positive reinforcement methods throughout this book, you now have everything you need to raise the dog of your dreams.

Now that you've started this journey of becoming a better parent for your pup, it's time to start consistently applying the tools you've gained throughout this guide.

Therefore, I'm going to end this book the same way it began, by **challenging you** to take these tools I've given you, and take the next step of applying them to your life on a daily basis! Like I tell all my private training clients, the best training in the world means nothing unless YOU consistently put in the work and practice immense patience!

🐾 WHERE TO NEXT?

My goal for writing this book was to cover 97% of the basic issues that are bound to arise when raising a crazy pup!

HOWEVER, there's bound to be that last 3% that you as a dog owner need additional guidance with... and, if you're really good, you're going to strive to fill that gap AND take your training skills to the next level beyond what was described in this book!!

The best way to do that is to follow me on all of my social media channels and dive into the free content I'm distributing there on a weekly basis! From my informational/how-to videos, vlogs and podcasts, I want to add as much value to everyone in the dog community as paw-ssible!

If you have ANY additional questions or inquiries, feel free to DM me on Instagram, Facebook, or Snapchat, or comment on one of my YouTube videos, and I'll get back to you ASAP (It's going down in the DM)!!

- ★ Instagram: https://www.instagram.com/**allthingspups**
- ★ Facebook: https://www.facebook.com/**allthingspups**
- ★ Snapchat: https://www.snapchat.com/add/**allthingspups**
- ★ Youtube: Search "All Things Pups" to find my channel :)

You can also submit an inquiry on www.allthingspups.com or reach me personally via email at kaelin@allthingspups.com.

With that, I sign off, wishing you nothing but a happy and well-behaved dog, to help you live a happy and more fulfilling life!

About the Author

KAELIN MUNKELWITZ

KAELIN MUNKELWITZ is the author of *The Puppy Training Handbook*, and founder of All Things Pups™, Southern California's premier dog training leader. With over 10 years and thousands of hours of dog training experience, Kaelin has quickly proved herself as a star in the dog training industry. She is the trusted trainer for many celebrities and influencers across the United States due to her extensive experience and uncanny ability to read and shape dogs' behavior through her fresh approach towards positive reinforcement training. With this book, it's her mission to help you improve your connection with your pup, and provide you with the tools to train any dog effectively and efficiently. For more information about Kaelin, check out her website at www.allthingspups.com.